Weapons of World War II (Infantry)

CONTENTS

LEFT: Two GIs man a foxhole with an M1 rifle and M1918A2 BAR. (NARA)

COVER IMAGES: Main image colourisation by ColourByRJM. (NARA) WEAPONRY: Images supplied by Denix Replicas (www.denix.es)

BELOW: A British soldier at Caen aims his Mo 4 Mk 1 rifle, July 1944. (IWM B6725)

ISBN: 978 1 83632 088 3
Editor: Chris Miskimon
Senior editor, specials: Roger Mortimer
Email: roger.mortimer@keypublishing.com
Cover Design: Steve Donovan
Design: SJmagic DESIGN SERVICES, India
Advertising Sales Manager:
Sam Clark
Email: sam.clark@keypublishing.com
Tel: 01780 755131
Advertising Production:
Becky Antoniades
Email:
Rebecca.antoniades@keypublishing.com

SUBSCRIPTION/MAIL ORDER
Key Publishing Ltd, PO Box 300, Stamford, Lincs, PE9 1NA
Tel: 01780 480404
Subscriptions email: subs@keypublishing.com
Mail Order email: orders@keypublishing.com
Website: www.keypublishing.com/shop

PUBLISHING
Group CEO and Publisher: Adrian Cox

Published by
Key Publishing Ltd, PO Box 100, Stamford, Lincs, PE9 1XQ

Tel: 01780 755131
Website: www.keypublishing.com

PRINTING
Precision Colour Printing Ltd, Haldane, Halesfield 1, Telford, Shropshire. TF7 4QQ

DISTRIBUTION
Seymour Distribution Ltd, 2 Poultry Avenue, London, EC1A 9PU
Enquiries Line: 02074 294000.

Infantry Weapons of World War Two

Introduction

Welcome to this special edition examining the various weapons used by soldiers around the globe during World War Two, the largest and deadliest conflict the world has yet seen. We look at the small arms and support weapons carried by the infantry and other ground troops of major combatant nations. Some will be instantly recognisable, while time has made others unfamiliar.

As with most wars, World War Two was fought with a mix of weaponry old and new at the time. Some soldiers carried rifles and machine guns created in the late 19th century. The German Mauser 98K (1898) and Soviet Mosin-Nagant rifle (1891) are just two examples of effective but dated designs. Other troops carried the latest models, such as the US M1 Garand and German StG44, the first practical assault rifle.

Whether aged or new, these weapons generally possessed several common characteristics. They had to be rugged and capable of standing up to field use. Reliability also ranked high; weapons that don't work are usually discarded by troops as soon as possible. Given the scale of the conflict, small arms also had to be mass produced, so simplicity of construction was another requirement.

Some of these weapons have faded into history, while others became iconic, having useful lives far beyond the conflict they were designed for. Even now, 80 years after the war ended, some of these weapons still appear on battlefields around the world. Mosin-Nagant rifles, PPSh-41 submachine guns and PM1910 Maxim machine guns have been seen regularly in the Ukraine war. Occasionally, weapons supplied to the Soviets through Lend-Lease make an appearance, such as American Thompson submachine guns. Leftover World War Two weapons are still often seen in Africa, the Middle East and Asia, alongside Armalites, Kalashnikovs and other more modern arms.

Each weapon is presented to the reader with its history, basic

BELOW: Two British soldiers advance cautiously into a Burmese town carrying their Short Magazine Lee-Enfield (SMLE) rifles. The soldier on the right has his spike bayonet affixed. (IWM SE2138)

BELOW RIGHT: Chinese troops were armed with a mix of Allied weapons. These troops have British SMLE rifles and a US M3 submachine gun. (NARA)

characteristics and illustrations of it in service. Where possible, descriptions of how each weapon was used are provided, including a few innovative ideas from troops in the field, preferably in the words of the veterans who carried, cleaned and slept next to them day after day. Some weapons had myths arise around them over time and where necessary these are explained or dispelled.

After the war, many of these weapons continued in service into the 1970s in some places, although major armies introduced new designs within a decade or two. It is a testament to their design, manufacture and sturdiness that so many examples lasted for decades after the war ended.

We hope you find this in-depth look at the firearms carried during humanity's most terrible conflict interesting. World War Two was a pivotal time in small arms development, as this selection of infantry weapons demonstrates. We have tried to find the photographs that show these weapons in field usage wherever possible, so please bear with the occasional grainy image. Camera quality varied back then, and sometimes the photographer was under fire!

ABOVE: A US machine gun team sets up a Browning water-cooled M1917 machine gun on high ground in Germany, 1945. (NARA)

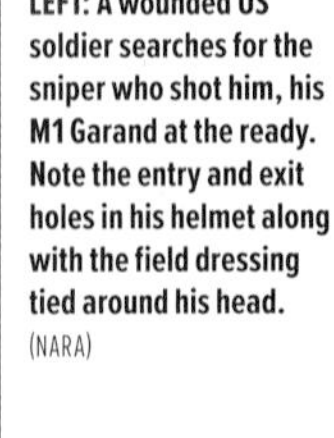

LEFT: A wounded US soldier searches for the sniper who shot him, his M1 Garand at the ready. Note the entry and exit holes in his helmet along with the field dressing tied around his head. (NARA)

LEFT: Soviet troops learn how to operate a Maxim M1910 machine gun under the watchful eye of a political commissar. The Maxim provided long-range fire support to Red Army infantry. (RIAN 668428)

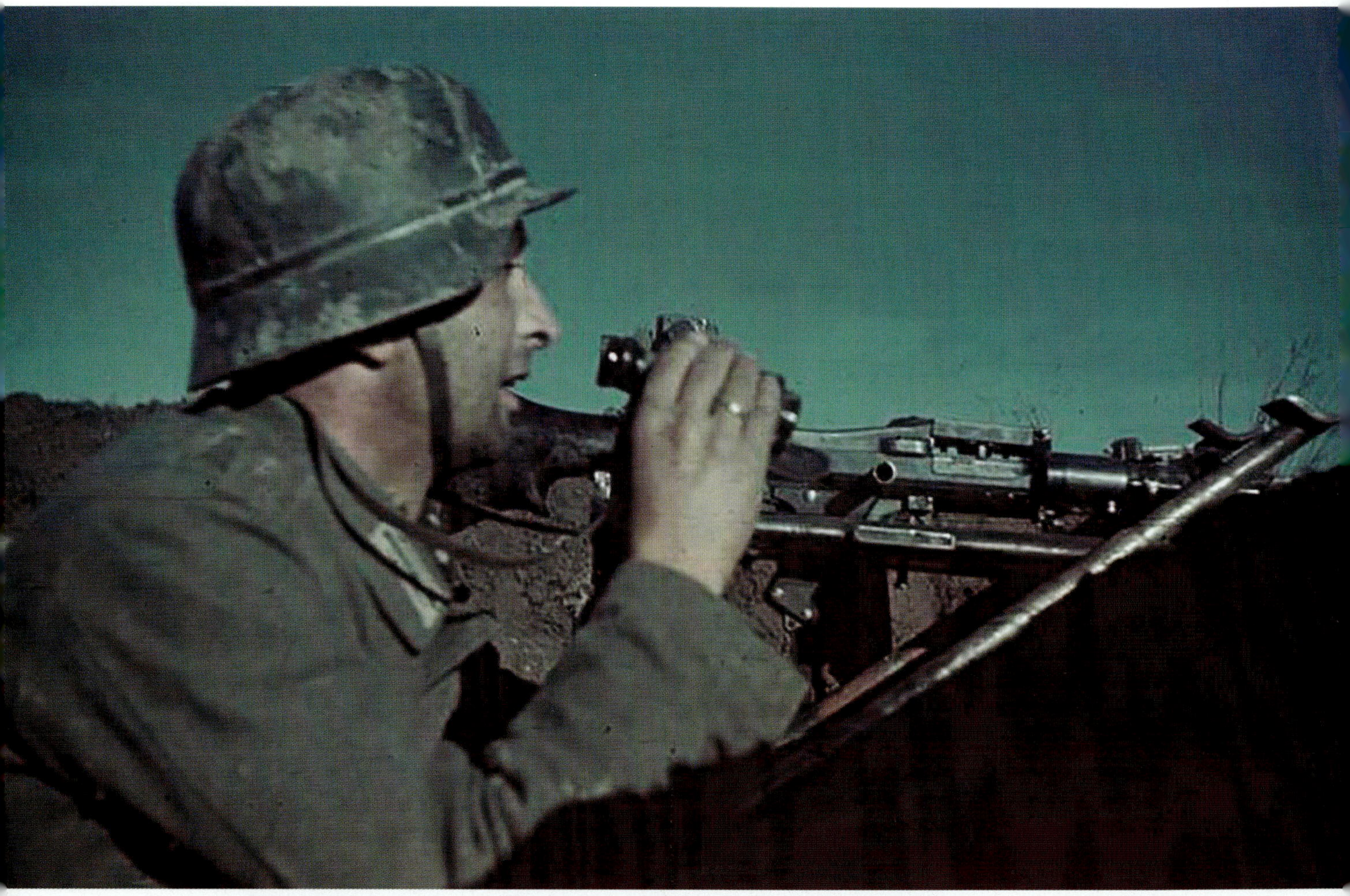

The Infantry in World War Two

Soldiers on the front line

ABOVE: A weary-looking machine gunner scans for targets at Stalingrad, 1942, next to a tripod-mounted MG34 machine gun. (BUNDESARCHIV BILD 169-0485)

RIGHT: This famous image shows three Red Army soldiers sharing a meal while a fourth stands guard with a DP-series light machine gun. His comrades have a rare Simonov AVS36 rifle and two more common PPSh41 submachine guns. (RIAN ARCHIVE 61150)

The infantry soldier has the toughest and most important job in any army. Tanks can smash through defences and artillery can shake the ground, but this is only to make way for dirty, tired infantrymen to seize and hold ground as only they can do. They close with and defeat enemy troops in close combat, sometimes even hand-to-hand. Infantry form the largest portion of frontline combat troops by number and they suffer a high proportion of casualties as a result.

This was as true during World War Two as it is today. The conflict saw industrialised warfare on a scale never before seen, occurring at numerous places across the world

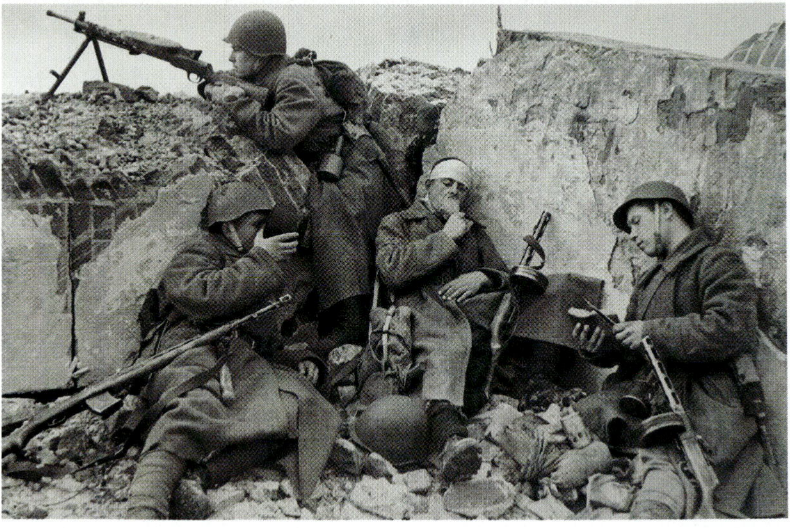

simultaneously. Everywhere fighting took place on land – Europe, North Africa, the Middle East, Southeast Asia, China and the Pacific Islands – infantry of all the combatant nations fought bloody battles against often bitter foes.

The weapons soldiers carried during the war rank among some of the most famous in history. Despite the war being 80 years past, books, documentaries and videos are still regularly produced about them. Video game designers who produce games depicting the war go to great lengths to accurately depict weaponry. Anyone interested in the war soon recognises names like Enfield, Mauser, Garand, Browning and Vickers. In the following pages, the reader will see these weapons and many others, running the gamut from pistols – at once the most useless and most coveted arm on the battlefield – to anti-tank weapons, which advanced greatly during the conflict. Of course, the standard weapon of the infantry is the rifle, with every other weapon enabling the riflemen to do their job of taking and holding ground.

However, the average infantry soldier carried more than just a rifle. A few hand grenades provided a hand-thrown explosive for fending off attackers or clearing buildings.

A squad might have a grenadier whose rifle was equipped to fire specialised rifle grenades and the others in the squad might carry a few rounds for more firepower. A few mortar bombs for the company or platoon mortar might go into their pack or maybe some ammunition for the squad's light machine gun (LMG). Almost all carried a bayonet, and these were often affixed to their rifle, but thankfully used much less often. Though only issued to leaders and soldiers assigned to crew-served weapons, many infantrymen tried to secure a pistol for the security it provided.

A few soldiers, such as squad and section leaders, might have a submachine gun (SMG) as they were useful at close range and when fighting in forests and towns. Specialised troops, such as airborne and commando units, might have more submachine guns since they were expected to see more close combat. The Red Army issued them widely for their firepower while the Japanese military hardly issued any. Since they tended to be compact, they were frequently issued to vehicle crews. However, most infantry units issued relatively few of them, far less than the number seen in most films. Later in the war, US Army

ABOVE: A posed photograph displaying the field kit of a Chinese soldier. Note the German-style helmet and four stick grenades in pouches. (US NAVY)

infantry companies were equipped with a few submachine guns at the company headquarters, to be issued when needed.

Machine guns, mortars and anti-tank weapons could be found anywhere from the squad up to weapons platoons and companies. Some armies issued small artillery pieces to infantry units, and unusual weapons such as shotguns and flamethrowers found their own uses.

Infantry organisation

How infantry weapons were used largely depended on how units were organised and the doctrine under which they operated. The basic infantry unit was the squad or section. A sergeant or corporal typically commanded them. Two to four squads made up a platoon, commanded by an officer, usually a lieutenant with a sergeant to assist. Table 1 shows how squads/sections, platoons and larger elements combined to make up an infantry battalion or regiment. Some organisations had machine gun or mortar sections within a platoon, though most nations organised these weapons into a weapons platoon-type grouping at the company level.

Battalions consisted of rifle companies, typically three or four, under a headquarters of company size or smaller. Machine guns and mortars were grouped into their own company or smaller groups to support the rifle companies. Regiments typically included three battalions with some nations including cannon or anti-tank companies at this level. Space precludes this publication from going into greater detail. Such organisation varied widely by nation and, »

Table 1. Basic Infantry Organisation during World War II	
Element	**Size**
Squad/Section	9-19 soldiers
Platoon	2-4 squads
Company	3-5 platoons with machine gun and mortars for support
Battalion	3-5 companies with supporting elements*
Regiment	3 battalions plus supporting elements

*these elements could include machine gun, mortar and sometimes infantry guns, plus logistics, communications and headquarters assets. Numbers and organisation depended on nation.

LEFT: Two soldiers of the US 145th Infantry Regiment man a bunker on Bougainville with a Browning M1917 30-calibre machine gun. The assistant has his M1 carbine at the ready. (NARA)

ABOVE: A Japanese soldier rises to throw his Type 97 hand grenade. Before throwing, the user had to strike the grenade on a hard surface, such as their helmet, to ignite the fuse. (IJA JAPAN PUBLIC DOMAIN)

RIGHT: A trio of German soldiers on a street in Hertogenbosch, Netherlands, 1944. The soldier with the Panzerfaust also has a captured US M1 carbine slung on his back. (POLISH NATIONAL ARCHIVES)

BELOW: A Marine on Iwo Jima lays down covering fire with a Thompson submachine gun; his mate has a Browning Automatic Rifle. The bolt on the Thompson is halfway from the full cocked position, indicating he has just pulled the trigger. (NARA)

during combat, units might reorganise for a specific mission or due to casualties. The German Army had many different types of infantry unit (infantry, airborne, panzergrenadier, volksgrenadier, volkssturm), all of which went through reorganisations during the war.

For the infantrymen, the squad/section was their home and family during the war, so Table 2 looks more closely at how squads were organised for different national armies. Most nations included some sort of light machine gun or automatic rifle at this level. Most nations also issued larger support weapons, such as heavy machine guns and mortars, at the company or battalion level.

Squad tactics

As seen in Table 2, most infantry squads had a light machine gun of some kind and a number of riflemen. While there are many tactics at the squad level, the basic one enabled by squad organisation is 'fire and manoeuvre', also known as 'fix and flank'. The machine gun team places fire on the squad's objective, suppressing the defenders, making it difficult for them to move or fire back. The riflemen can then move on the objective, preferably taking it from a more vulnerable flank. Part of the

Table 2. Typical Squad/Section Organisation by Nation

Nation	Size	Organisation
British Infantry 1944	10	Section commander (SMG), 3-man gun group with 1 Bren LMG and two rifles, rifle group with 6 riflemen
British Airborne 1944	10	Section commander (SMG), 3-man gun group with 1 Bren LMG, 1 Sten SMG and 1 rifle, 6-man rifle group with 1 SMG, 1 2-inch mortar, 4 rifles and 1 sniper rifle
US Army Infantry 1944	12	Squad leader and asst., with rifles, 3-man BAR team with BAR and two rifles; 5 riflemen, two were grenadiers using rifles with grenade launcher attachments
US Army Airborne 1944	12	Squad leader and asst., with rifles, 3-man MG team with M1919, 2 carbines and 1 rifle; 1 man with BAR; 6 riflemen
US Army Armored Infantry 1944	12	Squad leader and asst., with rifles, driver with SMG, 2-man rocket launcher team with rocket launcher and 2 rifles; 7 riflemen
US Marine Corps Infantry 1944	13	Squad leader with carbine, 3x4-man fire teams with 1 BAR, two rifles, two carbines each
US Marine Raider	10	Squad leader with rifle, 3x3-man fire groups with 1 SMG, 1 BAR, 1 rifle each
Soviet Infantry 1941	11	Squad leader with SMG, 2-man LMG team with DP27 and 1 rifle; 8 riflemen
Soviet Infantry Light Section 1944	9	Section commander and asst., 1x2-man LMG team with DP27, 5 riflemen. All might be armed with rifles, SMGs or a mix.
Soviet Infantry Heavy Section 1944	9	Section commander and asst., 2x2-man LMG teams with DP27; 3 riflemen. All might be armed with rifles, SMGs or a mix
French Infantry 1940	12	Group leader and deputy with rifles, 5-man fire element with 1 LMG, 1 pistol, 3 carbines; shock element with 5 riflemen, one with grenade launcher
Polish Infantry 1939	19	Squad leader and asst., with rifles, 4-man LMG team with LMG, 1 pistol and 3 rifles; 13 riflemen
Finnish Infantry 1940	10	Squad leader with rifle, 8 riflemen; 1 SMG gunner
German Infantry 1940	10	Group leader with SMG, 3-man LMG team with MG34, 2 pistols, 1 rifle; 6 riflemen
German Infantry 1944	9	Group leader and deputy with SMGs, 1x2-man LMG team with MG42, 1 pistol, 1 rifle; 5 riflemen
German Airborne 1944	10	Group Leader and asst., with SMGs, 2x2-man LMG teams with one MG34 or MG42 and 4 pistols; 3 riflemen, 1 sniper
Japanese Infantry 1944	13	Squad leader and asst., with rifles, 4-man LMG team with LMG, 1 pistol, 3 rifles; 7 riflemen
Italian Infantry	10	Squad leader with SMG, deputy with rifle, 3-man LMG team with LMG, 1 pistol, 2 rifles; 5 riflemen

squad is moving, the other supporting and covering.

In defence, the machine gun team formed the basis of the squad's defensive position. The riflemen guarded the machine gunner's flanks using rifle and rifle grenade fire and hand grenades if the enemy got close enough. Keeping the machine gun in action was important as it often inflicted more casualties on the enemy than the rest of the squad combined.

These tactics can be replicated at the platoon, company, and battalion levels, with increasing complexity and co-ordination requirements.

If mortars or artillery were available to support the infantry, even better. Anything that helped the infantry soldiers achieve their objectives at less risk to themselves was welcome. Supporting artillery fire, though beyond the scope of this work, was vital. According to one British infantry officer: "If I had to order my men to use their rifles I knew I hadn't got the level of artillery barrage correct." Allied troops generally had more artillery available and were happy to use it.

Keep in mind the weapons described in this special edition were used within the context of the squad, platoon, company, and battalion. Each soldier was a part of greater organisation, from regiment and brigade eventually up to the corps and field army. Each played their part in accomplishing the overall goal of seeking victory and ending the war. When needed, they used these weapons in anger against other human beings during the most terrible conflict the world has yet known.

LEFT: A mortar bomb explodes in front of a British Army signaller's jeep in Italy, September 1943. Mortars were effective indirect fire weapons for the infantry.
(IWM NA6857)

Pistols

A soldier's close personal friend

Pistols are the least useful of battlefield weapons due to their short effective range, low-powered ammunition and relative inaccuracy. They are also among the most coveted by soldiers, as they are compact, handy and provide a sense of security as a last-ditch emergency weapon they can keep with them at all times. Possessing a pistol is highly personal to a soldier for the feeling of protection it offers. Pistols are issued for various reasons as they do have practical purposes.

For officers and senior non-commissioned officers, pistols are a badge of authority and a symbol of their rank. In most of the World War

Two armies, someone carrying a pistol could be assumed to be a leader of some sort. For the infantry, this can be a liability as snipers and observant soldiers will target the enemy's leaders, taking note of someone waving a pistol around. Many leaders quickly learned to carry a rifle or carbine as well, which also made them better able to defend themselves in close combat.

A seldom discussed purpose for a leader's pistol was to maintain discipline in action. If a soldier displayed cowardice or fled in battle, an officer could shoot them to keep others from doing the same. Such things happened only rarely, even in armies that openly condoned such harsh measures.

Pistols were also issued to weapons operators, such as machine gunners, mortar teams and tank crews. These troops already had larger weapons to service so carrying a rifle and a useful amount of ammunition for it was impractical. For them, a pistol with a few spare magazines could be a lifesaver. Pilots and aircrew carried them in case they were shot down over enemy territory, as larger weapons would not fit in an already cramped cockpit.

Soldiers not issued pistols often went to lengths to acquire one. Many were not above stealing them; for example, US Marines who were about to perform an amphibious assault would break into the arms lockers of the naval transports they were aboard shortly before the attack, taking any pistols or other weapons deemed useful. In the field, captured enemy troops were of course searched and disarmed, with any pistols often kept by the capturing troops for personal use or as trophies.

Enterprising infantrymen often sold or traded captured pistols to rear-echelon troops whose duties behind the front lines prevented them from getting their own. US troops prized German pistols such as the Luger and

BELOW: Sgt James Nolan of the US 35th Infantry Division unloads his captured Walther P.38 pistol before going on pass at Nancy, France, in late 1944. (NARA)

P38, both for self-defence and because US laws regarding pistol ownership at the time allowed for weapons to be taken home as souvenirs. These wartime 'bringbacks' are now expensive collector's items in the US market.

Despite pistols being small and less powerful weapons, they did have their uses in specific situations. Troops used them in close-quarters combat, where the fighting distances could be measured in feet. This included urban fighting when troops advanced room-to-room or cleared tunnels. A handgun was also useful when clearing trenches or entering caves or bunkers. In close quarters, even carbines and submachine guns can be difficult to use, banging into walls or revealing the user's position because they project away from their body. Pistols can be kept close to the body, which also makes it harder for an enemy to grab them.

During World War Two, both revolvers and semi-automatic pistols saw wide use. At the time many considered revolvers more reliable, as some semi-automatic designs still suffered frequent malfunctions. Others preferred automatics, as most of the problems that will jam one are quickly corrected, while the issues that jam a revolver are fewer, but will often put it entirely out of action. Many nations used a mix of the two types.

The wide variety of pistols used during the war also highlighted the great demand for them. The United States issued no less than half a dozen different makes and models. The German military used several dozen different types, partly because their officers often provided their own pistols, but also because the Germans adopted weapons from occupied nations to make up for production shortfalls of the Walther P38. The combatant nations produced tens of millions of pistols during the war to keep up with the demand.

ABOVE: US soldiers go through a box of surrendered German sidearms shortly after the war's end. It is likely that all these pistols would have gone home as souvenirs. (PATTON MUSEUM)

ABOVE LEFT: US Army Private James Pickett, just freed from a prisoner of war camp in April 1945, posed comically with various seized items, including Polish Radom or Tokarev and a Browning P.35 pistols, both issued to German troops. (NARA)

LEFT: US General George Patton was known for carrying flashy pistols as part of his carefully cultivated image. Here he decorates a soldier while carrying his famous Colt Peacemaker; his other preferred weapon was a Smith and Wesson .357 Magnum revolver. (NARA)

Enfield No 2 Mk 1

After World War One, the British military decided to acquire a replacement for the large .455 Webley Mk VI revolver. The Webley served well overall, but was heavy and hard for some soldiers to handle due to its size and recoil.

The result, adopted in 1932, was the Enfield No 2 Mk 1, which largely resembles a scaled-down Webley, as both are topbreak designs where the upper frame and cylinder rotate away for loading and ejection of the spent cartridge cases. Webley in fact contributed to the design, although there was a dispute as to how much so, resulting in a lawsuit. The government later compensated Webley. When the war began there was not enough Enfield revolvers available, so Webley's design was issued as a substitute standard.

Enfield No 2 Mk 1	
Calibre	.380
Capacity	6-round cylinder
Length	10.25in (26cm)
Weight	1.7lb (.767kg)

In 1939, the British army adopted the No 2 Mk 1* which operated in double action mode only, where the weapon's hammer could not be cocked and could only be fired through a long pull of the trigger. The Mk 1* lacked a hammer spur as it was not needed on a double action-only revolver. The spur could also snag on clothing or equipment when drawn from the holster. Most Enfields were produced to this standard or converted to it during the war. It is rare today to find one in the original configuration.

As using a pistol at anything beyond a few yards takes extensive training and practise, the British Army sensibly trained its largely conscripted force in fast, double action shooting at short ranges. As such, the Enfield proved effective. Some Commonwealth troops preferred the Smith and Wesson revolver, but that was mostly a matter of personal opinion. The author's Mk 1* is accurate to 25 yards and is very controllable in rapid fire. While it lacks the smooth trigger of a Smith and Wesson, it is easy to use effectively.

This capability proved useful to a tank crewman of A Squadron, 3rd Carabiniers, serving in Burma in 1945. During fighting in broken terrain, a sword-wielding Japanese officer climbed aboard the tank, killed the tank commander and dropped into the turret, killing the 37mm gunner as well. The loader, Trooper Vernon Jenkins, shot the enemy officer several times with his revolver, but the crazed man kept fighting. As they wrestled atop the bodies of the commander and gunner, Jenkins managed to grab another revolver from the gunner's holster and put two more shots into the Japanese officer's head, finishing him. Jenkins received a Military Medal for his courage.

The Enfield continued in British service after the war until the 1960s.

Colt M1911A1

The venerable .45

The venerable Colt Model 1911 series is the iconic American military handgun. The US Army developed the weapon in the early years of the 20th century, wanting a powerful handgun able to stop attacking enemies after experience in the Philippines against Moro guerrillas. After adoption in 1911, it quickly became the standard handgun for the entire US military, serving in World War One and undergoing improvement in the 1920s, afterward known as the M1911A1 (for 'Alteration 1').

Unusually, the pistol incorporated three separate safeties; a half-cock notch in case the hammer slipped during operation, a grip safety that prevented the pistol from firing if not firmly grasped in the shooter's hand, and a thumb-actuated safety for use when the weapon had a round in the chamber and a cocked hammer. In practice, many soldiers carried it with an empty chamber, requiring them to cycle the slide when needed. This method was slower but safest as there is no round in the chamber until ready to fire.

The US government purchased almost two million M1911A1s during the war, in addition to those previously

Colt M1911A1	
Calibre	.45 ACP*
Magazine	7 rounds
Length	8.6in (21.9cm)
Weight	3lb (1.36kg)
*Automatic Colt Pistol	

in service. Five different companies produced them, and they were widely issued. The pistol was generally popular with US troops, although some complained they could not shoot it well (pistols are more difficult to learn to use than rifles). Most GIs referred to the pistol simply as the 'forty-five'.

In British service, the .45 was frequently issued to commandos, paratroopers and the SAS. The famed SAS officer 'Paddy' Mayne carried one and used it to save the life of a Sergeant Major Rose. An Italian soldier was about to shoot Rose in the back when Mayne drew his .45 and shot the enemy soldier down with two well-placed rounds. "Be careful Mister Rose" was all Mayne said afterwards.

American troops made frequent use of the weapon. Corporal Henry Warner of the 1st Infantry Division earned a

Medal of Honor for using his .45 to drive off a German tank by shooting at the tank's commander standing in the top hatch. Ralph Carmichael, also of the 1st Infantry Division, carried one in Normandy. He rounded the corner of a hedgerow one day and ran into a German soldier. "I didn't know if he was waiting to ambush us, but I didn't wait to see," Carmichael said. "I shot him with my pistol... The .45 was a very effective round."

ABOVE: A sergeant keeps his .45 at the ready after he and another soldier shot two Germans while clearing out snipers near St-Lo, France, in July 1944. (NARA)

LEFT: A soldier of No. 9 Commando prepares to go on a patrol at Anzio with his M1911A1. Note the lanyard attached to the pistol and around the commando's neck to prevent loss of the weapon if it was dropped in action. (IWM NA12472)

Smith and Wesson Revolvers

ABOVE: Even Axis forces used the popular Smith and Wesson, including this Vichy French member of the Milice, a militia-police group, guarding captured French Resistance members in 1944. (BUNDESARCHIV 101I-720-0318-36)

American manufacturer Smith and Wesson is famous for its sturdy and reliable revolvers and many of them served during the war. These weapons were frequently used by police forces worldwide at the time and it was only natural they would follow into military service. Officers and others who could furnish their own pistols often opted for some sort of Smith and Wesson, particularly those who found the Colt .45 M1911A1 unsuitable for them.

These revolvers were six shot models, which came in several different calibres, depending on the user or issuing military organisation.

UK Commonwealth forces issued hundreds of thousands of them, mostly in .38/200, known in the US as .38 S&W. American troops used them in either .38 Special or .45 calibre. Two major types made up most of the numbers in service:

The Victory Model. These are medium frame weapons in .38 calibre, either the British .38/200 or the .38 Special cartridge popular in the United States. Four or five-inch barrels were most common, though they could vary anywhere from two to six inches. Commonwealth users often preferred them to the standard Enfield due to their solid construction and smooth trigger pull. They had a reputation for functioning in rough conditions even with little maintenance. They are often referred to as the Model 10 or the 'Military and Police'.

Many Victory models saw issue to pilots and clandestine agents due to their lighter weight. Commonwealth troops often had them at the front lines, but they were rarely issued to American combat units. However, some US troops managed to get hold of them and used them in action. US Marine Raider R G 'Rudy' Rosenquist carried one and used it at Guam. He later wrote (in the third person): "Now a second enemy soldier came running, and Rudy took a bayonet wound in the stomach. By this time, he had got out a .38 pistol, which he emptied into the man, who fell back upon the Marine at the machine gun…"

Model 1917. Some American troops carried a larger-framed Model 1917 revolver in .45 calibre. These pistols were produced during World War One due to a shortage of .45 automatics at the time. Placed in storage after the war, the government reissued the big M1917 during World War Two as well. It fired the same ammunition as the M1911A1, but used small clips to allow loading of the .45 cartridge, which was designed for use in automatic pistols.

RIGHT: A private in the US 1st Cavalry Division cleans his M1917 .45 revolver in the Pacific. The pistol has a lanyard loop on the butt, though US troops rarely used them. (NARA)

Smith and Wesson revolvers		
	Victory Model*	**M1917**
Calibre	.380	.45ACP
Capacity	6-round cylinder	6-round cylinder
Length	10.125in (25.7cm)	10.8in (27.4cm)
Weight	1.94lb (.88kg)	2.25lb (1.02kg)

*In American use, the Victory Model used the .38 Special cartridge.

Soviet Pistols

Simple but durable

The Red Army issued two primary pistols during World War Two, one a revolver and the other a semi-automatic. Both saw wide usage with troops and partisans. Given the brutal nature of the Soviet Union during the war, there are dark jokes that Soviet pistols were more often used for executions than combat. However, pistols were issued in the Red Army to leaders, weapons crews and vehicle crews just as in any other army. German troops used captured examples as they did other Soviet arms.

Nagant Model 1895. This revolver pre-dates the communist regime and was designed by Belgian Leon Nagant. It is a 'gas seal' design; as the cylinder turns, it moves against the barrel's forcing cone to make a rough seal. The ammunition is designed with the bullet recessed into the cartridge case to help make this seal. The purpose is so less gas escapes during firing. In practice it was unnecessary. There was a double action version for issue to officers and single action for enlisted soldiers. It was issued with a holster that also carried seven spare rounds of ammunition.

In service, the M1895 had a terrible trigger pull, took a long time to load and was needlessly complex. However, it proved durable and was available in large numbers. It is estimated about two million were produced by the end of World War Two.

Tokarev TT33. This semi-automatic design entered production in 1936. It fires the same ammunition as the PPSh41 and other Soviet-era submachine guns. Like the Nagant, it is simple and rugged. Wartime examples were often crudely finished, but the weapon was reliable. About 1.6 million were made by 1945. The Germans captured enough to put it into service as a substitute pistol for their own troops, using 7.62mm Mauser pistol ammunition, which would function in the Tokarev.

Soviet troops found pistols just as useful as other soldiers during the war. Three German soldiers captured a young Soviet private named Timofey Bogrov when they leapt into his trench before he could reach his rifle. When the Germans turned away from him for a moment, he drew his M1895 from a pocket and killed all three. Soviet snipers often carried them as a close-range defence weapon and some scouts carried them for trench raids or in urban areas where they might suddenly meet an enemy at close-quarters.

ABOVE: Soviet troops advancing early in the war, possibly during the Winter War with Finland. The man in the foreground has a Nagant M1895 revolver. (NARA)

LEFT: An iconic image of a young Soviet officer leading his troops, waving his Tokarev TT33 pistol to beckon them forward. Note the lanyard tied to his holster. (RUSSIAN ARCHIVES)

Soviet Pistols		
	Nagant M1895	**Tokarev TT33**
Calibre	7.62 Nagant	7.62x25mm
Capacity	6-round cylinder	8 rounds
Length	9.07in (23cm)	7.68in (19.6cm)
Weight	1.75lb (.795kg)	1.83lb (.83kg)
Note: Ammunition for these weapons was not interchangeable		

ABOVE: German soldiers on the Eastern Front, 1942. These soldiers appear to be clearing a town; one keeps his P.08 at the ready. (POLISH ARCHIVES)

Pistole P.08

The famous Luger

Pistole P.08 Luger	
Calibre	9mm Parabellum
Magazine	8 rounds
Length	8.75in (22.2cm)
Weight	1.92lb (.877kg)

German designer George Luger's name is forever attached to this pistol and while he did aid in development and patented the weapon, the original design was by Hugo Borchardt, another German weapons designer of the late 1800s. The German army adopted it in 1908, and it served throughout World War One in various versions. German troops referred to the weapon as the Pistole P.08 and do not appear to have ever called it a Luger. The pistol production occurred at the DWM and Mauser factories; there never was a manufacturing plant named for Luger, who was an employee of DWM.

Rather than operating with a slide mechanism as most other pistols, the P.08 uses a toggle link that hinges upward when the pistol cycles after firing, ejecting the spent cartridge case before moving back down and forward to load a fresh round. This made the weapon complicated to produce, with tight tolerances in its machining. This also led to higher production expenses, which contributed to the weapon's official replacement as the standard service pistol by the Walther P.38 in the late 1930s. Despite this, it stayed in production through 1945, as the demand for pistols exceeded the supply of P.38s and every other pistol the Third Reich issued to make up for the shortfall. Enough spare parts remained at the factory and elsewhere after the war that small numbers of P.08s were assembled through the 1980s.

Despite its complexity, the weapon was generally reliable and performed well in field use. The standard 9mm calibre was sometimes supplemented by civilian-market pistols in 7.65mm (.32). P.08s were issued with a clamshell-style holster that completely enclosed the weapon, protecting it from the elements. These holsters also carried a spare magazine and sometimes a cleaning rod. Soldiers liked the P.08 and many kept them instead of the standard issue P.38.

The pistol pointed well, meaning the shooter could simply extend the weapon towards a target and the barrel would usually be aligned on it. The quality of its construction also kept it popular; with regular maintenance it could be expected to perform.

The P.08 was perhaps most popular with Allied soldiers, who usually referred to it as the Luger. The pistol was sought-after as a souvenir, largely because it was a quintessentially German weapon. German troops were aware of this and occasionally left booby-trapped P.08s behind for unwitting Allied troops to pick up. This did not deter American troops from taking back tens of thousands of them to the United States, where they remain prized collector's items.

RIGHT: This British Commando officer caries an 'artillery' model P.08, with a longer barrel and a 32-round 'snail drum' magazine. (IWM H14599)

Walther P.38

The German military had no problem with the performance of the P.08 Luger but nevertheless adopted the P.38 because the P.08 was expensive and complex to produce. The P.38 officially replaced the P.08 as the standard sidearm on April 26, 1940. Once in service, troops liked it as it featured the latest in pistol technology, including a double action trigger and a safety that dropped the hammer, allowing the weapon to be carried with a round in the chamber.

It also featured a loaded chamber indicator just over the hammer on the slide. When there is a cartridge in the chamber, a small pin protrudes from a hole, allowing the user to quickly ascertain whether the weapon is ready to fire. Even in the dark, a soldier can simply feel for this pin with their off hand. Late-war production models sometimes lack this feature as the rush to produce pistols more quickly led to its omission.

The German military issued the first P.38s to tank crews, as the Panzer branch was popular with Hitler. Most were made by Walther and Mauser, issued with a holster holding a spare magazine and a cleaning rod. Production was never enough to replace all the other pistols the German military issued, but the P.38 was the official standard. Total production is hard to determine, but somewhere around one million P.38s were produced during the war.

Soldiers found the P.38 accurate and dependable and its 9mm cartridge more effective than the smaller calibres found in many of the ad hoc-issue pistols Germany used, such as the 7.65mm. It was also very popular with Allied troops, both as a souvenir and a fighting handgun. One source states US troops always wanted P.08s as souvenirs but kept P.38s handy for actual use in combat. Like the P.08, thousands were taken back to the US after the war, making them popular collector's items to this day.

Walther P.38	
Calibre	9mm Parabellum
Magazine	8-round box
Length	8.6in (21.9cm)
Weight	2.12lb (.96kg)

ABOVE: A young German paratrooper in Tunisia carries a P.38 and stick grenade tucked in his belt along with his Mauser rifle. (BUNDESARCHIV BILD 101I-788-0009-13A)

LEFT: A US soldier relieves a captured German officer of his P.38 pistol. Note the weapon's safety is in the 'on' position. (NARA)

Pistols in Action

Pistols saw wide use by soldiers of all the combatant nations. Frontline troops often kept one on their person for emergencies or close combat. In action, it was often quicker to draw a pistol than reload their primary weapon. This could make the difference between life and death during a battle. These images showcase the variety of pistols in use during the war.

ABOVE: Two British soldiers rush past a burning home in France, August 1944. The lead soldier carries a revolver at the ready, useful in close-range fighting.
(IWM B8587)

ABOVE RIGHT: German soldiers pause during the Ardennes Offensive, December 1944, probably to smoke the cigarettes they have just captured. The man on the left holds a Browning M1935, a 9mm pistol with a 13-round magazine.
(BUNDESARCHIV)

RIGHT: Japanese troops in China, 1939. The seated officer brandishes a Nambu pistol.
(IJA-PUBLIC DOMAIN)

ABOVE: A Soviet partisan leader shows his men how to operate a Browning M1935 pistol, likely just captured from a German soldier. Pistols were valuable to partisans for their ease of concealment. (RIAN #965)

FAR LEFT: A Chinese soldier carrying a Mauser C96 variant in Shanghai, 1937. Chinese troops favoured the Mauser pistol design. This soldier's cartridge belt is made for the weapon. (US NAVY)

LEFT: A French Resistance Fighter strikes a dramatic pose, a Beretta Model 1934 tucked in his belt. The Beretta was the standard officer's pistol in the Italian Army. (NARA)

BELOW LEFT: This SS soldier has a captured Soviet Nagant revolver tucked into his cartridge belt and secured with a chain lanyard. The Nagant was not a good weapon, but was better than no pistol at all. (NARA)

BELOW: A line of British soldiers from 7th Battalion, Green Howards, advance in Tunisia, April 1943. Their officer has a Smith and Wesson revolver ready. (IWM NA1277)

Submachine Guns

ABOVE: The Thompson submachine gun was well known to the American public and frequently used in propaganda artwork. (US ARMY)

back, extracting the spent cartridge casing and feeding a new round for firing. This continues until the user releases the trigger and the bolt stops cycling until the trigger is squeezed again.

The open bolt mechanism, sometimes referred to as a blow-back design, is simple and reliable. It is lightweight and easy to produce in large numbers. Open bolt designs tend to be less accurate due to the movement of the bolt, but since submachine guns fire pistol rounds, they are short-range weapons anyway. While they can be effective out to 200 metres or so in expert hands, on average 50 metres is more realistic for an average shooter under the stress of combat.

After World War One ended, several designs intended for the trenches were refined into practical weapons that served through World War Two. This included an improved MP18 and the Thompson. They joined inter-war weapons, such as the MP38/40 and Suomi Model 1931, along with wartime productions including the Sten, M3 'Grease Gun' and PPSh41.

These weapons were manufactured in the tens of millions and saw wide service in all theatres of the war. Only the Japanese army made limited use of them, though that

The submachine gun is a creation of World War One, though the type saw only limited service in that conflict. The most prominent of these initial models was the German MP18, which saw use in the trenches during the last few months of the war. Its simple design provided the basic pattern for a submachine gun for the next four decades.

A submachine gun is a fully automatic weapon, more compact than a rifle or carbine, which fires a pistol-calibre cartridge. The models of this era fired from an open bolt; the firer charges the weapon by cocking the bolt to the rear, where it stays held in place until the trigger is squeezed, the sear pin drops, and a spring pushes the bolt forward. This strips a cartridge out of the magazine and into the chamber, where it is fired. The recoil forces produced by firing push the bolt

RIGHT: Two British paras man a radio post in Holland, February 1945. One stands watch with his Sten at the ready. (IWM B14347)

was partly due to the limits of their manufacturing capability after the war began. The submachine gun offered short-range firepower, good for close assaults, urban fighting and jungle warfare.

The Soviets equipped entire battalions with them for close assaults; hundreds of troops could lay down a heavy if inaccurate fire while hundreds more advanced or manoeuvred. The Red Army needed vast numbers of small arms and their easily and quickly produced submachine guns were widely issued.

Airborne units also made extensive use of submachine guns and issued them beyond the normal allocations. Their relatively light weight, high magazine capacity and firepower made them good for the aggressive close attacks paratroopers carried out.

However, for regular troops, submachine guns saw more limited issuance than is often portrayed in films and fiction. Usually, no more than one soldier per infantry squad would have one, at most. Many soldiers preferred the longer range of a rifle, so submachine guns were often kept in reserve and issued when needed. Tank crews often had a submachine gun or two for personal defence; infantry would borrow them when clearing towns or bunkers.

While the rifle remained the prime infantry weapon, submachine guns proved versatile and useful in many situations, which guaranteed they remained in service through the war and beyond. They were only replaced as frontline weapons post-war by the rise of the assault rifle.

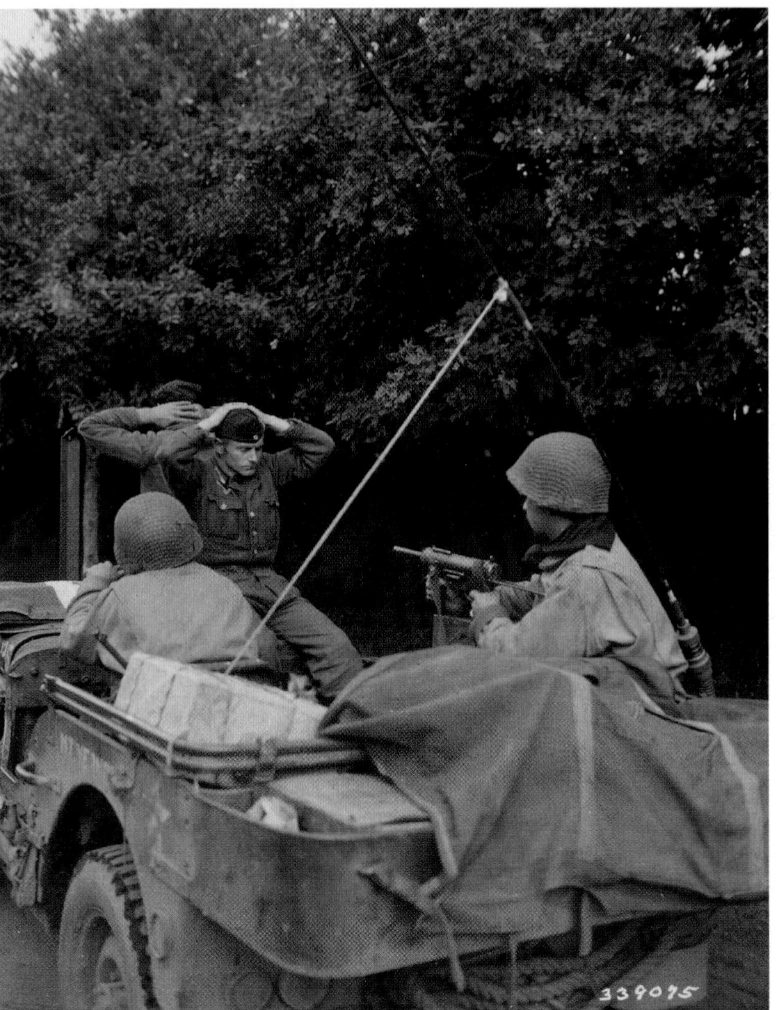

ABOVE: In March 1945, two soldiers of the 1st Royal Norfolk Regiment take aim. One is using a captured German MP40. (IWM B15048)

ABOVE LEFT: A Finnish soldier uses a reindeer to carry supplies for his unit, keeping his Suomi submachine gun at hand. This weapon has the stick magazine inserted. (SA-KUVA)

LEFT: A US GI covers two prisoners with his M3 'Grease Gun'. US troops commonly put prisoners on the hood of a jeep to make any nearby enemy soldiers reluctant to fire at them. (NARA)

Sten

RIGHT: Two Canadian soldiers display a Nazi flag they captured in Normandy. The soldier on the left has a Sten, probably a Mark II. (LIBRARY AND ARCHIVES CANADA)

BELOW: Two lance corporals guard a road intersection near Ranville, France, June 7, 1944. Each is armed with a Mark V Sten. (IWM B5291)

The British Sten gun was a marvel of wartime expediency, even among the mass-produced weapons of the Second World War. Its name is an acronym, combining the first letters of the last names of the weapons designers, Major Reginald Shepherd and Harold Turpin, with the first two letters of the Enfield factory, where it was first produced. The Sten filled a gap in British small arms at a desperate time. Just after the Dunkirk evacuation, the threat of German invasion loomed large, and Britain needed all the weapons it could get. The nation needed a weapon that could be manufactured quickly, cheaply and be simple to operate.

The Sten met these criteria. Most of its parts were stamped, with only a few requiring complex machining. It shared some characteristics with the Lanchester submachine gun, itself a copy of the German MP28. This included the side-mounted magazine, which fed from a double column to a single column for firing. This arrangement made the magazine more susceptible to dirt and bent feed lips, leading to some of the Sten's reliability problems. Stens were much faster to produce than the Lanchester, whose production rate averaged about 3,400 weapons a month. The BSA factory at Tyseley could make 47,000 Stens per week!

Four major versions of the Sten saw service, with the others being experimental or special-purpose models. The Mark I and Mark I* were the initial models, with about 300,000 made. The simplified Mark II could be made faster and could be quickly disassembled for paratroopers. The magazine well could also be rotated downward to make the weapon easier to store; when in the down position, it also served as a dust cover for the ejection port. This was the most common Sten type, with about 2.6 million produced. The Mark III contained even fewer parts and was designed to be even faster to produce. It was often issued to the

British Home Guard and dropped to resistance groups. More than 876,000 Mark IIIs left the production lines.

In January 1944, the Mark V entered production. Many experts consider it the best Sten model to be made in large numbers. It had a wooden stock and pistol grip. Initial models also had a forward pistol grip, but it had problems and was eliminated. The Mark V's quality was markedly better than previous types, but it also took longer to make and was more expensive. Production ended in May 1945 with about 500,000 made. Suppressed version of the Marks II and V saw service with British Special Forces, commandos, resistance groups, the SOE and the OSS.

Once in service, the Sten drew praise and criticism from users. Reliability issues were the worst complaint. Some troops did not care for its ugly appearance, nicknaming it the 'Plumber's Helper' or the 'Stench Gun'. If the weapon were dropped on its stock, even with the bolt closed, there was a chance of the Sten firing unintentionally.

In combat, the Sten proved capable despite its shortcomings. Para Lt Richard Smith, carrying a Mark V, took part in the seizure of the Orne

Sten Mk II	
Calibre	9mm Parabellum
Magazine	32-round box
Length	30in (76.2cm)
Weight	8.16lb (3.7kg)
Rate of Fire	550 rpm

River and Canal Bridges on D-Day, June 6, 1944. While leading his troops over one of the bridges, a German threw a grenade at him and then tried to escape by climbing over a wall. Smith said: "I shot him as he was going over – I made certain, too. I gave him quite a lot of rounds, firing from the hip – it was quite close range."

The Paras used their Stens again during the ill-fated Operation Market Garden in Arnhem. Signalman Bill Jukes of 2nd Parachute Battalion used his when an attacking column of German armoured vehicles crashed in front of his position. He wrote: "Those of us with Stens joined in the general fusillade. One of the radio operators grabbed my Sten... but I snatched it away from him, telling him to get his own. I hadn't waited five years to get a shot at the enemy like this only to be denied by some Johnny-come-lately to the section. It was impossible to say what effect my shooting had. There was such a volley coming from the windows along the street that nobody could have said who shot who."

Stens saw wide use in all theatres of the war along with thousands more air-dropped to resistance fighters. Some resistance groups even made their own Stens in hidden workshops. They continued in post-war use into the 1950s with the British military and are still in use around the world. So many were made they continually appear in conflicts, including new production ones based on the original designs. US Special Forces used them in Iraq and Afghanistan, where their compactness made them useful for shooting from inside a vehicle.

ABOVE: This famous image shows four British paratroopers moving through a damaged house in Oosterbeek, Holland, during the fighting around Arnhem. Two are armed with Mark V Stens while the other two have a semi-automatic pistol and a revolver. (IWM BU1121)

BELOW LEFT: A trio of British soldiers occupy a foxhole in anticipation of a Japanese counter-attack in Burma, January 1945. They have the three main infantry weapons of the British Army: a Bren light machine gun, a Lee-Enfield rifle, and a Sten gun. (IWM SE2374)

BELOW: A French Resistance fighter with a Sten during the liberation of France. As Allied troops advanced, local French fighters often joined them, providing information about the enemy in the area. (NARA)

Thompson

designs were desired for use on the Western Front. American Army officer John T Thompson designed his submachine gun for trench clearing, but the war ended before he could finish the design. He marketed it to police departments instead, where it saw wide use by criminals and police during the gangster era in the United States. The US military adopted it formally in 1928, though initially it did not buy the weapon in large numbers.

These first models, the M1928 and M1928A1, saw wide issue to Allied armies in the early years of the war, but not because it was perfect for their needs. Rather, it was the only SMG in widespread American production, and thus the only thing available. Troops generally liked them for their firepower, though it required regular maintenance in cold, desert or jungle climates.

The M1 Thompson appeared in 1942 as a simplified production model. This included a simplified rear sight, the removal of the compensator on the barrel and the use of a straight wooden fore-end rather than the pistol grip often (but not always) used on the M1928. Some M1s were fitted with compensators, likely in the field. An even simpler model, the M1A1, entered production in 1942. The easiest way to differentiate between an M1928 and an M1/M1A1 is that the cocking handle on the M1928 is on top of the upper receiver while on the M1/M1A1 is on the side. Also, the M1s cannot use the 50-round drum magazine, which saw little military use anyway because the rounds noisily rattled inside it in field use.

The US military purchased the M1 and M1A1 in larger numbers as the production simplifications dropped the price from $225 for an M1928 to $44 for an M1. British and Commonwealth units used the M1928 initially, but also

The Thompson submachine gun ranks among the most well-known weapons of World War Two. It saw service with practically every Allied nation. The United States, the UK and most Commonwealth armies used it as their primary submachine gun until war expedient models such as the Sten, M3 and Owen appeared. Even then, many troops kept their Thompsons, preferring them to the rougher wartime types. Even the Soviet Union received some under Lend-Lease, though they were not optimal for the Red Army and most went into storage. Interestingly, some of those have seen use in the Russia-Ukraine war that began in 2022.

The Thompson originated in the final days of World War One, when various light automatic weapon

acquired M1s and both models served throughout the war. Thousands were supplied to Nationalist Chinese forces, who liked them so much they began to produce copies of the M1, some of which later appeared during the Korean and Vietnam conflicts.

On March 4, 1941, British Commandos carried Thompsons during their raid on the German harbour in the Lofoten Islands. One commando reported: "A burst would lift a man off his feet. No one hit by those bullets ever put up any further resistance." The commandos liked the Thompson so much that when it was scheduled for replacement by the Sten, Sgt Jack Lovell said: "We went mob-handed to the CO and said if we couldn't keep the Tommy guns, we'd all transfer back to our [previous] units." The Thompsons stayed.

US Marines in the Pacific found an effective way to pair the Thompson with the larger BAR during patrols. The lead soldier (the 'point man') used a Thompson loaded with tracer rounds while the second man carried a BAR. When the point man saw a target and opened fire, the BAR man looked for the tracers and directed his fire in the same direction. This allowed a Marine squad to direct heavy automatic firepower in the first crucial seconds of an engagement.

In Europe, US troops loved their Thompsons, generally preferring them over the M3 Grease Gun just as

British soldiers often preferred them over the Sten. US infantry squads were not normally issued submachine guns, but a few always found their way into soldiers' hands, where they were particularly useful in urban combat. One veteran told the author: "The problem with the Thompson was that you usually found a reason to use it," putting the man carrying it up front. He also said that when moving

through German towns and cities, ammunition supply was problematic simply because the Thompson went through so much of it.

The Thompson's high quality of manufacture, dependability and power made it stand out against the lower quality production weapons like the Sten and M3. It was much heavier and cost far more, but troops loved it and kept them through war's end.

ABOVE: A British Army corporal unloads M1928 Thompsons from a Lend-Lease shipment in March 1942. The M1928's high manufacturing standards made it sturdy and well-liked by those lucky enough to get one. (IWM H18068)

ABOVE LEFT: A GI in the 148th Infantry Regiment fires his M1 Thompson at attacking Japanese on Bougainville. The weapon's power and rate of fire were useful in jungle fighting. (NARA)

LEFT: A fusilier of the Royal Scots ready to lay down covering fire with his M1 Thompson in Burma, October 1944. Note he has the magazine pouch for holding six 20-round magazines for his weapon. (IWM SE2989)

M1 Thompson SMG	
Calibre	.45
Magazine	20/30-round box
Length	32in (81.3cm)
Weight	10.45lb (4.74kg)
Rate of Fire	700rpm

M3 Grease Gun

America's Sten gun

RIGHT: Soldiers of the Brazilian Expeditionary Force, which served in Italy, hold a position. They frequently equipped entire patrols with the M3 for the firepower to break contact. (BRASILIAN ARCHIVES)

The M3 is the American version of the British Sten gun; rough but simple, inexpensive and easy to manufacture. In 1941, several examples of the Sten arrived in the United States for testing, with an eye toward producing a similar weapon for its own rapid military expansion. This makes the M3 essentially a derivative of the Sten.

With such a firm start on development, examples of the new M3 were ready for trials just before the attack on Pearl Harbor. The weapon used metal stamping in most of its construction, with only a few machined parts, such as the barrel. Its tubular appearance quickly earned it the nickname 'Grease Gun' due to its resemblance to the automotive tool. Production cost of an M3 was $20.94 at the time, half the cost of an M1A1 Thompson.

In service, problems arose due to its rushed production. The cocking handle broke easily, the sights were bad and it lacked sling swivels. Most of its problems were addressed in an improved version, the M3A1, which eliminated the cocking handle. Instead, a user inserted a finger into a recess in the bolt and pulled it back until the sear engaged. A hinged dust cover swung down to keep out dirt and

a small pin on the cover held the bolt in place once cocked, providing a simple safety. The Grease Gun fired only fully automatic. A skilled user can fire single rounds by fast trigger manipulation due to the weapon's low rate of fire.

The M3 could convert to 9mm calibre through a conversion kit, though only a small number were made. This kit used a Sten magazine. The Office of Strategic Services (OSS), in charge of arming covert operatives and guerrillas, ordered a few M3s with an integral suppressor produced by Bell Laboratories. Stories of their use in World War Two are

scant, but they remained in service with US Special Operations Forces into at least the 1980s.

In service, the Grease Gun's reputation was mixed. Many soldiers preferred their Thompsons, but some appreciated the M3's simplicity and size. They were often issued to tank crews and others who needed a compact weapon or one with good short-range firepower.

One unique use of the Grease Gun was told to the author by a GI who served in the US 157th Infantry Regiment. When his unit was clearing German towns, they would often run out of grenades. If that happened, they borrowed a Grease Gun from a supporting tank crew. The trigger was wired back so the weapon would fire as soon as the bolt was cocked. With the bolt in the forward position, a magazine was inserted. The lead soldier crept up to the doorway or window of the room to be cleared, pulled the bolt back and threw the entire weapon into the room. Inside, the Grease Gun would fly around the room, firing in all directions from the uncontrolled recoil until the magazine became empty. The veteran assured me no one would stay in a room with a chattering, jumping Grease Gun!

BELOW: Two GIs shoot the lock on the gate of the Hammelburg POW camp in April 1945. This is probably posed for the photographer based on the lack of concern from the onlooking soldier. (NARA)

M3 'Grease Gun'	
Calibre	.45 ACP
Magazine	30-round box
Length	29.33in (74.5cm)
Weight	10.25lb (4.65kg)
Rate of Fire	350-450 rpm

Owen

Officially known as the Owen Machine Carbine, the Owen gun served the Australian Army well during World War Two and stayed in service until the 1960s. Its designer, Evelyn Owen, was serving as a private in the Australian Army when he designed the weapon. Initially, some in the Australian military establishment opposed adoption of the Owen, preferring to wait for the arrival of the British Sten gun. However, testing of both weapons along with some other submachine guns showed the Owen to be at least as reliable and accurate as any of them. It entered production in 1942 and 45-50,000 were made at an approximate cost of $30 each.

The Owen has several unusual design features and externally has a simple appearance similar to the Sten. The magazine fed from the top of the weapon, sticking straight up from the receiver. This allowed gravity to help the magazine feed fresh rounds into the weapon during firing. This feature required the sights to be offset slightly to the side, making aiming more difficult, though many users simply fired from the hip. The ejection port sat at the bottom of the receiver, so spent cartridge cases simply fell out the bottom. This also allowed any dirt, mud or water that entered the weapon to be easily drained out the bottom.

Once in service, the Owen proved itself to be very sturdy and dependable. Most users preferred it to the Sten and Thompson, saying it was more reliable than either weapon. Australian troops nicknamed it the 'Digger's Darling'. New Zealand soldiers also used the Owen and gave it high praise, too. The US Army evaluated the Owen and considered purchasing 60,000 of them, but the production capacity and raw materials to build so many were lacking.

In the field, Owens were the preferred weapon for patrols due to their compactness and ease of handling. Many of the weapons were painted in a camouflage pattern at the factory as it was known it would see service in the South Pacific. The only criticism made about the Owen concerned its weight. However, that helped absorb recoil, keeping the weapon steadier on target.

Owen Gun	
Calibre	9mm Parabellum
Magazine	33-round box
Length	32in (81.3cm)
Weight	10.6lb (4.82kg)
Rate of Fire	700 rpm

BOTTOM: A soldier from the 2/43rd Battalion moves cautiously forward at Labuan, June 1945. Many soldiers tucked the Owen's stock under their arm to hold the weapon solidly while firing from the hip. (AWM)

BELOW: An Australian soldier of the 2/3rd Battalion near Kalimboa village in New Guinea, April 1945. The selector lever just above the trigger is forward, set to full automatic fire. (AWM)

Suomi KP31

Finland's deadly submachine gun

Suomi KP31	
Calibre	9mm Parabellum
Magazine	30 or 50-round box, 70-round drum
Length	34.25in (87cm)
Weight	15.52lb (7.04kg)
Rate of Fire	900 rpm

ABOVE: A Finnish soldier peers over the barrel of his Suomi during the fighting on the Karelian Isthmus in July 1944. The Suomi was an excellent weapon for close fighting in forests. (SA-KUVA)

The Finnish Suomi KP31 is one of the lesser-known submachine gun designs of World War Two, but experts consistently rank it as one of the best weapons of its day. The KP31 entered service in 1931. It is usually referred to as the 'Suomi', which simply means 'Finnish', in effect calling it the Finnish submachine gun.

The Suomi's construction was high quality, with a lot of precision machining and a full wooden stock. It used either a 50-round box magazine or a 70-round drum. It was often used as a light machine gun, as its high manufacturing standards and design made it accurate even at long range for its 9mm pistol cartridge. A Suomi-equipped soldier sometimes had an assistant gunner who carried spare magazines.

During the Winter War between Finland and the Soviet Union, the Suomi gained a fearsome reputation in the hands of the aggressive Finnish troops, who used skis to quickly move around the flanks of Soviet units and launch ambushes or isolate them. Afterwards, small groups of Finnish soldiers with Suomi submachine guns launched raids and small attacks to inflict casualties and break enemy morale.

There were so many stories of Finnish submachine gunners inflicting heavy casualties that journalists began to underreport the numbers, afraid readers would not believe them. P T Kekkonen wrote: "Nobody can believe my eye-witness's claim that one submachine gunner can slaughter 85 enemy soldiers during a skirmish lasting less than 30 minutes!"

During one Soviet attack, hungry Red Army troops stopped after capturing a Finnish field kitchen and helped themselves to the rations. Two Finns formed a team, one with a flashlight, the other with a Suomi. When the flashlight lit up a group of Soviet soldiers, they froze like a deer in a car's headlights. The Suomi gunner then cut them down.

In December 1941, the famous Finnish soldier Lauri Torne (later known as Larry Thorne) found a platoon of Soviet soldiers while on a reconnaissance mission. Rather than withdraw, he attacked them with his Suomi and a few hand grenades, wiping out 48 troops. It was a common Finnish tactic to launch a surprise attack with grenades, following up with submachine gun fire and snipers targeting the officers. With the Soviet position in chaos, the attackers quietly withdrew.

Finnish sniper Simo Hayha holds the grim record of killing the most enemy soldiers during a war, at 705. While he mostly used a Mosin-Nagant rifle, he killed more than 200 people using a Suomi, usually in forested terrain where he could get close enough make his shots count. The Suomi was so effective and well-liked it served the Finnish military until the 1980s.

RIGHT: Clutching his Suomi, a Finnish soldier takes cover in a trench system during an enemy barrage in June 1944. They may be expecting an infantry assault, as his comrade holds a grenade at the ready. (SA-KUVA)

PPS43

Simple Soviet firepower

The Soviet Union embraced the submachine gun more than any other combatant nation during the war. While its most numerous submachine gun design was the PPSh41, the PPS43 comes in second with two million produced. Like the more numerous PPSh, the PPS43 is simple, easy to manufacture, use and maintain.

While the Red Army liked the PPSh, its need for weapons was so great it wanted something even simpler, which could be produced more quickly, at lower expense and using fewer raw materials. In particular, the PPSH had a long, fixed, wooden stock that made it harder for vehicle crews to store, and it was heavy. The PPS43, designed by Alexei Sudayev, won the competition for the new weapon, having several key features, including a metal folding stock, so no wood was used at all. It was also lighter and made extensive use of metal stampings to quicken production time. The PPS43 used half the steel and weighed much less; a PPS43 could be made in 2.7 hours. Production goals were set at 350,000 per month.

The initial version of the weapon was called the PPS42. It went into production in 1942 at the Sestroryetsk Arsenal near Leningrad. The first weapons saw combat in December. Some minor design improvements came out of that field testing, with an improved model called the PPS43. It proved rugged and reliable. As it had a folding stock, it was often issued to vehicle crews and was ideal for paratroopers and others who needed a compact and lightweight weapon for close combat. The PPS43 saw widespread issue to Soviet troops and many wartime photographs show them armed with the PPS43 and PPSh41 in the same photograph, so it appears the weapons were issued in mixed groups. German troops used captured examples and Finland copied it directly as did other nations like China after the war.

ABOVE: PPS43-armed Soviet soldiers fire at retreating German troops in the city of Krasnoye Selo, January 1944. This town is just south of Leningrad and near a factory that produced the weapon. (RUSSIAN ARCHIVES)

Perhaps the finest compliment paid to the PPS43 came from Mikhail Kalashnikov, who designed the famous AK47 rifle. He called the PPS43: "The best submachine gun of the World War Two period. Not one foreign design could be compared with it in simplicity of construction, reliability, durability in function, and ease of use. Airborne troops, tankers, scouts, partisans, and ski troops loved the Sudayev weapon for its... combat qualities, combined with its small dimensions and weight."

PPS-43	
Calibre	7.62x25mm
Magazine	35-round box
Length	31.8in (80.8cm)
Weight	8.6lb (3.9kg)
Rate of Fire	700 rpm

BELOW: A motorcycle unit of the Red Army's 1st Czechoslovak Corps, with machine guns mounted on the sidecars. The drivers have PPS43 submachine guns slung across their chests. (RUSSIAN ARCHIVES)

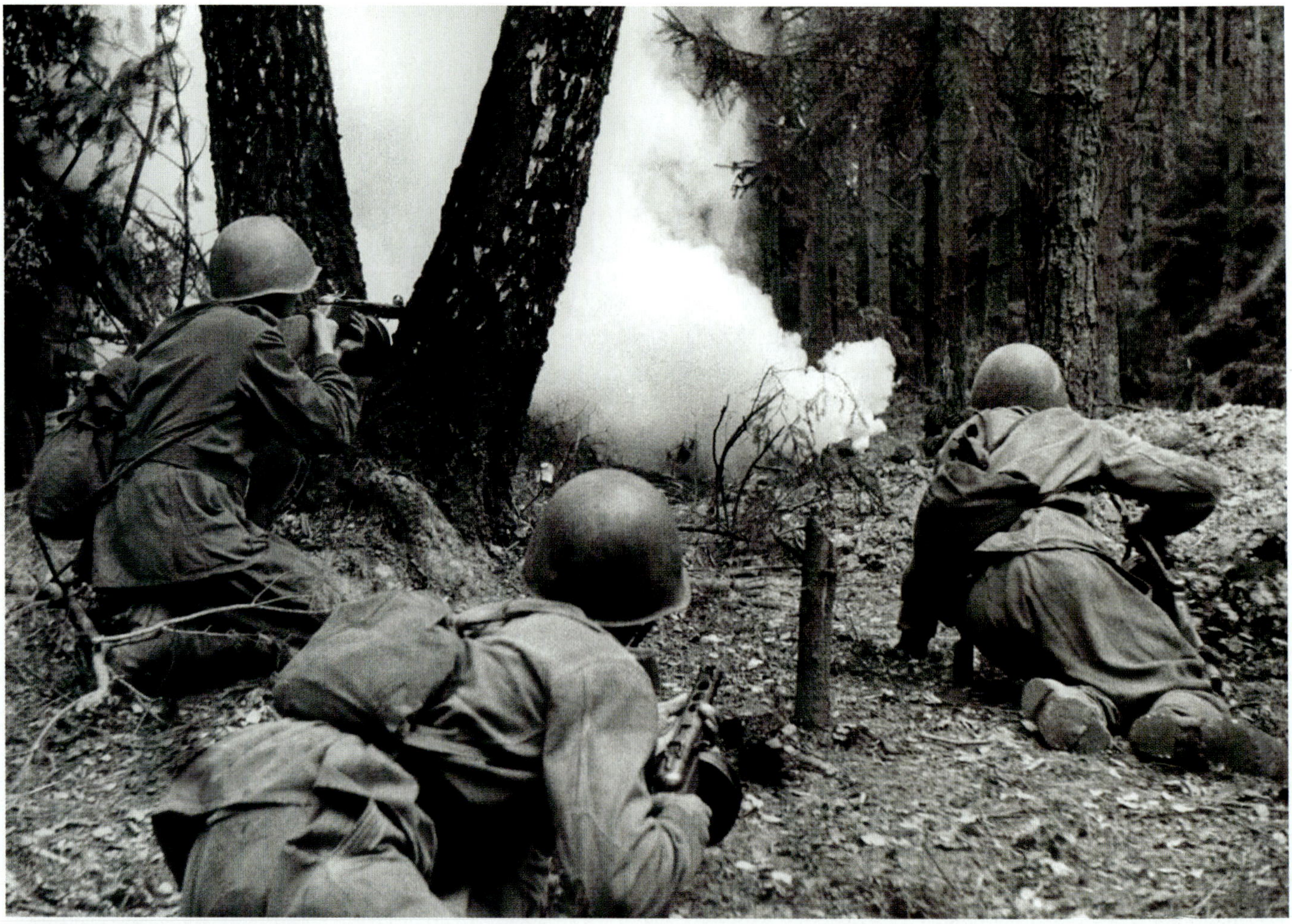

PPSh41

The most widely issued Soviet automatic weapon

ABOVE: A smoke grenade billows in front of PPSh41-armed Soviet troops of the 1st Belorussian Front near Warsaw in 1944. (RUSSIAN ARCHIVES)

RIGHT: This German soldier on the Eastern Front in 1943 has armed himself with a captured PPSh. The drum magazine provided good firepower for a close-range firefight. (BUNDESARCHIV_BILD_101I-276-0702-33)

The PPSh41 submachine gun is the iconic Soviet weapon of World War Two. Widely issued during the conflict, eventually 25% of Soviet soldiers were issued a submachine gun, and most of those were this famous model, known as the 'Pa Pa Sha,' the Russian pronunciation of the Cyrillic letters P, P and Sh in the model designation. The Soviet Union produced more than five million PPSh41s by the end of the war, and more after.

Red Army troops suffered heavy casualties during the Russo-Finnish Winter War of 1939-40. Many of these losses occurred at the hands of Finnish infantry armed with Suomi submachine guns. This taught the Soviet military the value of a good submachine gun and led them to

further their own designs past the existing PPD40, which was a decent weapon but not suitable for mass production. Needing vast numbers of them to equip their tough but poorly educated conscripts, they sought a simple, rugged design. After testing, the Red Army adopted a design by one of its soldiers, Georgy Shpagin.

In true Soviet fashion, the new PPSh41 was crude, but simple and dependable. It was a straightforward blowback design firing from an open bolt, as most submachine guns. Shpagin strove to make it easy to manufacture, made mostly of stamped metal parts welded together. This allowed the weapon to be produced quickly and cheaply in either large factories or small local workshops. It took 5.6 hours to make one weapon. A standard barrel for a Mosin-Nagant rifle could be cut in half to make two PPSh barrels.

In the field, the PPSh41 proved easy to operate and maintain by Soviet infantry. It could be quickly field-stripped and cleaned to keep it in action during heavy fighting. It used either a 71-round drum magazine, popular for its firepower, or a 35-round stick magazine, which was lighter. In practical terms, it was effective out to 200m for an experienced user.

The Red Army issued submachine guns on a vast scale, more so than

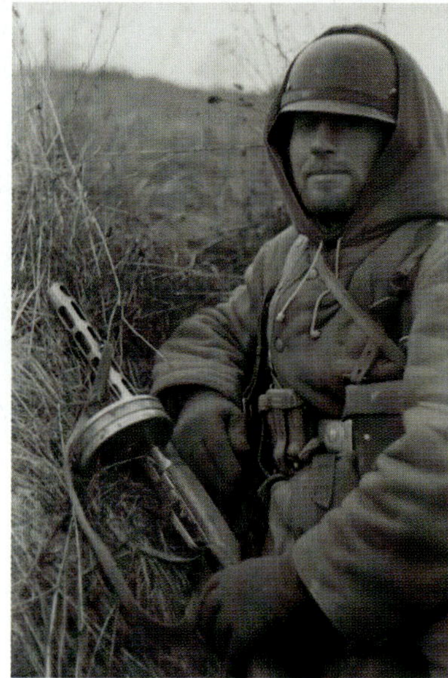

any other combatant army. At the beginning of the war, Soviet rifle regiments had a submachine gun company with three 31-man platoons. Later in the conflict, the Soviets expanded the allocation of submachine guns and even had battalions and regiments armed with submachine guns for shock attacks. By 1943, Soviet tank brigades included a battalion of submachine gunners. These troops protected the tanks from close infantry assault. Known as 'tankodesantniki', or tank riders, they rode the tanks into battle and jumped off when enemy forces were encountered. Even the 'riflemen' in Soviet infantry squads often carried submachine guns.

The PPSh proved so effective in combat and reliable even in cold weather the Germans made use of captured weapons. This happened at the tactical level when individual soldiers took up captured weapons to use until their supply of captured ammunition ran out. The Germans also captured large numbers of weapons and issued them, designating it the MP171(r), with the letter r standing for Russian. The Germans issued 7.62x25mm Mauser ammunition with these weapons, as it would work in unconverted PPSH41s.

They also converted many PPSh41s to 9mm calibre, with an adaptor so it could use the MP40's magazine. This conversion was called the MP41(r).

Soviet troops generally liked the PPSh41. Since the Germans excelled at using artillery and other long-range weapons, Soviet troops often tried to get within 50m or so of German

ABOVE: Soviet troops fighting in an Eastern European village. Note, all the troops appear armed with the PPSh41. (RUSSIAN ARCHIVES)

PPSh41	
Calibre	7.62x25mm
Magazine	35-round box or 71-round drum
Length	32.6in (82.8cm)
Weight	11.9lb (5.4kg)
Rate of Fire	900 rpm

troops to nullify this advantage. At this distance the PPSh was very effective, able to put down heavy fire to suppress or kill enemy troops. At Stalingrad in 1942-43, Soviet assault groups used PPSh41s and grenades for close-quarters urban combat.

Sniper teams often carried a PPSh for close fighting when needed. At Sevastopol in 1942, sniper Sgt Mariya Baida used a PPSh to attack a German position. After creeping up to the position she cut down 16 Germans with her submachine gun, including the German officer. She even used the butt of the weapon to strike down several enemy soldiers. During her assault she captured a German machine gun and liberated nine captured Soviets, including her commanding officer.

During the battle for Berlin in April 1945, Lt Evgeni Bessonov used a captured German submachine gun, to his regret. He later wrote: "Right in front of me was a Fritz in a trench. I tried to cut him down with my German submachine gun, but... some sand had got into the bolt. I jerked the bolt, pulled the trigger, but it did not fire. The German did not think long, grabbed his rifle and aimed at me... a submachine gun burst sounded in the air and the German dropped dead at the bottom of the trench. It turned out it was Drozd who cut him down with a Soviet PPSh submachine gun, which never jammed in battle. Why the hell did I carry that German submachine gun?"

LEFT: Submachine guns like the PPSh41 were useful in urban fighting, where ranges were usually short and the ability to fire bursts at sudden targets was an advantage. (RUSSIAN ARCHIVES)

LEFT: These Soviet troops occupy a trench along the crest of a hill. Note how the nearest two soldiers are holding the drum magazine for their weapons, keeping them from hitting the ground and being damaged. (RUSSIAN ARCHIVES)

MP40

Germany's standard submachine gun

The MP40 is another of the most famous weapons of the war. It is instantly recognisable, largely because they were so often seen in World War Two films in the hands of almost every German soldier seen on screen. In reality, German infantrymen were issued the weapon much less frequently than seen on film, with submachine guns normally only issued to squad and platoon leaders.

The weapon is an evolution of the MP38, which looks overall very similar. The MP38 used metal stamping and other simple manufacturing techniques to make it quick to produce. It was still a quality weapon and with its folding stock was frequently issued to armoured vehicle crews and paratroopers. The MP40 succeeded it as a further simplified model to allow even faster manufacture. The weapon could be assembled at a central factory from parts made in small workshops. Both

weapons are often referred to as 'Schmeissers', but German weapons designer Hugo Schmeisser did not design the weapon. However, he had

a hand in several other designs, so his name seems to have simply been attached to it. Most German troops referred to it as 'MP', short for the German word for a submachine gun, machinenpistole.

The MP40 proved popular in service. Though only capable of fully automatic fire, its rate of fire was slow enough to make the weapon controllable. A skilled user can snap off single shots if needed. It was simple to use and maintain; the weapon and its 9mm ammunition were not heavy, allowing a user to carry a good amount without being burdened.

Allied troops often captured MP40s, which proved useful for urban combat. British troops could use their own ammunition in the weapon, although American and Soviet troops had to rely on captured supplies. Although Soviet troops were liberally supplied with their own submachine guns, many images exist of red Army troops using them. Oddly, German troops preferred to use captured Soviet SMGs on the Eastern Front because they were more reliable in the cold. This can also be attributed to the tendency of all soldiers to overvalue their opponents' weapons, particularly since they have been on the receiving end of them. Partisans also used them when available.

In practice, users gripped the MP40 with one hand on the pistol grip and the other on the lower receiver

RIGHT: A young German soldier poses with his MP40 on the Eastern Front in January 1944. (BUNDESARCHIV_BILD_101I-278-0899-26)

BELOW: A German soldier uses his SMG to take a prisoner, 1941. This is likely a posed picture as the German has no magazine in his weapon. (BUNDESARCHIV_BILD_146-1974-099-39)

just in front of the trigger guard or more often by the magazine well, which is doctrinally the correct way. Firing them with one hand gripping the magazine is largely another Hollywood invention, as gripping it that way could induce malfunctions.

After 1941, when the Germans encountered the large number of SMG-armed Soviet troops on the Eastern front, they began to issue two SMGs per squad. Late in the war, when Germany started to form units with less time for training, entire squads and platoons might be issued SMGs as it took less training to learn to use one. Germany produced around 1.2 million MP38s and MP40s before and during the war and also used other designs, including captured weapons often rechambered for 9mm.

MP40	
Calibre	9mm Parabellum
Magazine	32-round box
Length	32.8in (83.3cm)
Weight	10.36lb (4.7kg)
Rate of Fire	500 rpm

The MP38 and MP40 saw extensive combat service. When Germany invaded the Netherlands in May 1940, the German Special Forces unit known as the Brandenburgers used them for a covert mission. Two Brandenburgers dressed as Dutch military police appeared at a railroad bridge, escorting six German 'prisoners', each with an MP38 with the stock folded, concealed under their uniforms. Using surprise, they quickly overpowered the Dutch troops guarding each end of the bridge and secured it for a German armoured train to cross.

The famous Soviet sniper Vasiliy Zaitsev mentioned using the German submachine gun in an unusual night attack. After using a knife to silence a sentry, Zaitsev and his comrades crept quietly into a German bunker and found a group of German soldiers, all asleep. Several MP40s were hanging on pegs on a nearby wall, so the Soviet soldiers grabbed them and opened fire on their sleeping enemy, killing them all in seconds.

SS soldier Emil Werner of 12th SS Panzer Division owed his life to a comrade with an MP40 during the fighting in Normandy. His company had already taken casualties while moving forward. As he and his comrades moved through some woods, Werner recalled: "SS-Grenadier Grosse of Hamburg jumped behind me towards some bushes with his submachine gun pointed, shouting, 'Hands up!' Immediately, two British soldiers out with their hands raised."

After the war, thousands of MP40s found their way onto battlefields across the world. The Allies distributed many captured and seized weapons as military aid. Even in the 21st century, they still appear in the hands of insurgents in Africa and the Middle East.

LEFT: A 16-year-old boy soldier in the Volkssturm in October 1944. He carries a well-worn MP40. (BUNDESARCHIV_BILD_183-J28021)

ABOVE: Simone Segouin, a French partisan who became famous after a series of photographs were taken of her in 1944. She is demonstrating her firing stance with her MP40, which was a correct one for hip-shooting at the time. (NARA)

LEFT: A German paratrooper in action with his MP40 in Italy in 1943. Note the cartridge cases in the snow near the weapon. (BUNDESARCHIV_BILD_101I-571-1707-08A)

Submachine Guns in Action

Submachine guns saw extensive use worldwide. Even soldiers who prized their rifles understood the value of them in the right circumstances. Experienced soldiers often displayed a preference for the higher quality pre-war designs then the wartime expedient models like the Sten. On these pages the reader can see some lesser-known types as well as a few more interesting images of the more famous SMGs.

LEFT: An Italian paratrooper talks to some German airborne troops at Anzio in April 1944. He has a Beretta Model 38 slung across his back. Many consider this one of the best SMGs of the war. The vest carries spare magazines. (POLISH ARCHIVES)

BELOW LEFT: This British Army photo shows a Japanese Type 100 SMG, made in small numbers. Standard Japanese practice put a bayonet on everything from SMGs to light machine guns. (BRITISH ARMY)

BELOW: A Finnish soldier uses a captured Soviet PPD40 with the little-seen curved box magazine. It was more often seen with a drum magazine. (SA-KUVA)

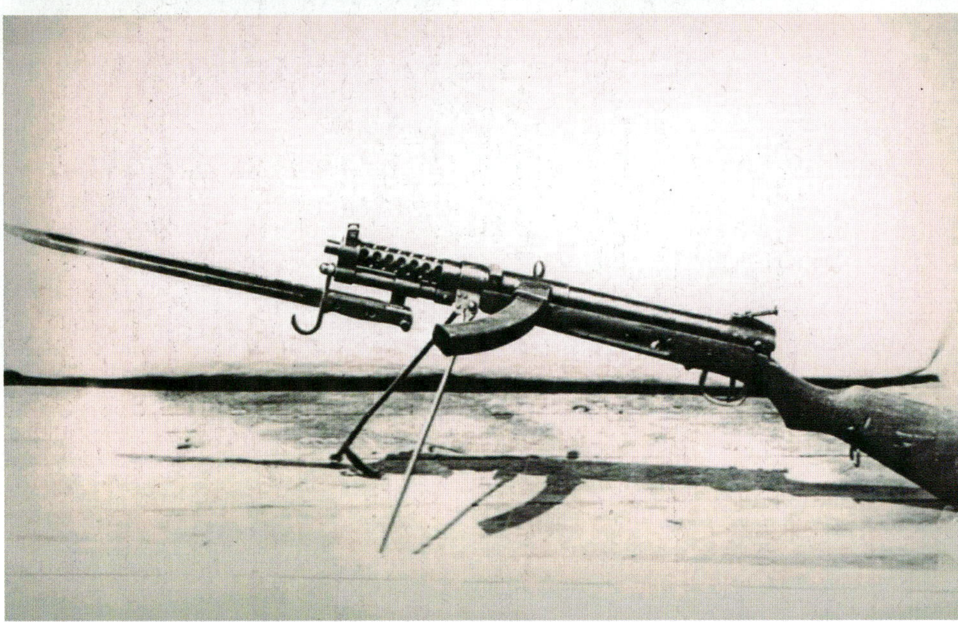

ABOVE: A Soviet partisan commander demonstrates how to operate a captured German MP38. Partisans used whatever weapons came into their possession. (RUSSIAN ARCHIVES)

LEFT: A Dutch soldier fires an M1928 Thompson with a 50-round drum magazine. Note the blur of the cocking handle as it moves atop the weapon. (DUTCH NATIONAL ARCHIVES)

BELOW LEFT: Soviet sailors raise their banner over Port Arthur, August 1945. They carry a mix of PPSh41 and PPS43 SMGs. The PPSh held by the soldier in the rear has a box magazine instead of the famous drum magazine. (RIAN 834147)

BOTTOM: SS troops in action, 1942. The soldier on the right has an MP28, a pre-war design often used by the SS and rear-echelon troops. (BUNDESARCHIV)

BELOW: The Reising SMG came in fixed or folding stock versions. It was used by the US Marines in the Paçific, but soon removed from service due to poor reliability. (NARA)

Rifles

The rifle is the main weapon of the infantry soldier. It provides the best balance of portability, accuracy, range and power. Whatever other weapons frontline soldiers carried – pistols, submachine guns, machine guns or grenades – the rifle is what they used more than any other weapon. In most armies, every soldier, when a new recruit, learned how to use a rifle, whether they went on to serve in the infantry or not.

RIGHT: A Finnish infantryman in a fighting position with his Mosin-Nagant rifle. Finland inherited thousands of these rifles when it became independent and later made its own version of this Russian design. (SA-KUVA)

BELOW: A German sniper with his scoped Mauser takes aim on the Eastern Front, March 1943. His spotter is using his field glasses to assist. (POLISH ARCHIVES)

World War Two saw a variety of rifles in action, as each major combatant nation generally produced its own model. In particular, rifles demonstrate the technological advancement of the time. Many soldiers carried the same rifles their fathers and even grandfathers carried in World War One and earlier.

These were universally bolt-action weapons, which require the firer to manually work the bolt between each shot. Bolt actions are strong, able to handle high-powered rifle cartridges, as opposed to lever or pump-action types. They are also simple to maintain and operate. Bolt action rifles gained ascendancy in the late 1800s and were the mainstay infantry rifle through World War Two in terms of numbers and types in service.

However, World War Two saw the ascendance of the semi-automatic rifle. Work on various designs during the 1920s and '30s resulted in several working models that served during the war, most famously the US M1 Garand. There were also less well known weapons such as the German G41, G43 and FG42, along with the Soviet AVS36 and SVT40.

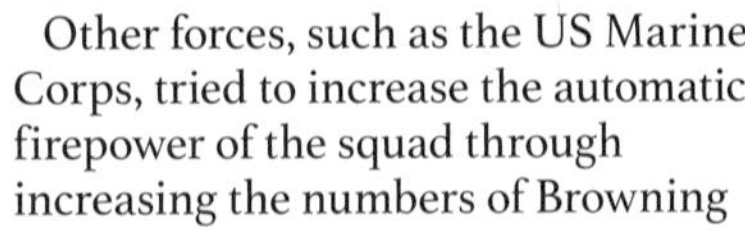

Unlike submachine guns, semi-automatic rifles generally fire from a closed bolt, which cycles from the energy produced by the gases of the cartridge being fired. Closed bolt weapons are more accurate for ranged fire and the semi-automatic rifle's lower overall rate of fire reduces the chance of overheating.

The war also introduced the assault rifle, the standard infantry weapon today. Assault rifles fire what is often referred to as an intermediate cartridge, less powerful than a full rifle round, but more powerful than pistol ammunition. Only one real model arose during the war, the German Sturmgewehr 44, but it set the stage for post-war development.

The assault weapon concept took hold because the weapon could be used for semi-automatic or controllable, fully automatic fire. Intermediate cartridges had a lower maximum effective range, but this proved no real hindrance as most infantry combat took place at ranges of up to 300 metres, so full powered rifle rounds were not needed. Squad machine guns like the MG42 still fired the full powered round, and German infantry squads were centred around the machine gun anyway.

Other forces, such as the US Marine Corps, tried to increase the automatic firepower of the squad through increasing the numbers of Browning Automatic Rifles (BARs – see page 64), but did not have an assault rifle design during the war. In fact, US forces had no such weapon until the 1960s; the German military led the way in this respect. Fortunately, the internal politics of the Third Reich prevented the weapon from getting into service earlier.

The development of semi-automatic and assault rifles changed the role of the infantryman from that of an individual marksman to part of a team putting out heavy firepower. Combined with portable light and general-purpose machine guns, the infantry squad was no longer just a collection of riflemen, but a vital and powerful part of the combined arms team.

ABOVE: A New Zealand corporal takes aim with his scoped SMLE at the Battle of Cassino, Italy, March 1944. (IWM NA13384)

LEFT: Surrendered German soldiers turn in their rifles in 1945. There are a few Mauser 98ks and what appear to be crudely made 'Volkssturm' rifles issued in desperation late in the war. (NARA)

BELOW: A bayoneted rifle stuck muzzle-first into the ground marked the grave of many soldiers during the war. Though grim, it allowed Graves Registration troops to recover the body after the fighting. (US NAVY)

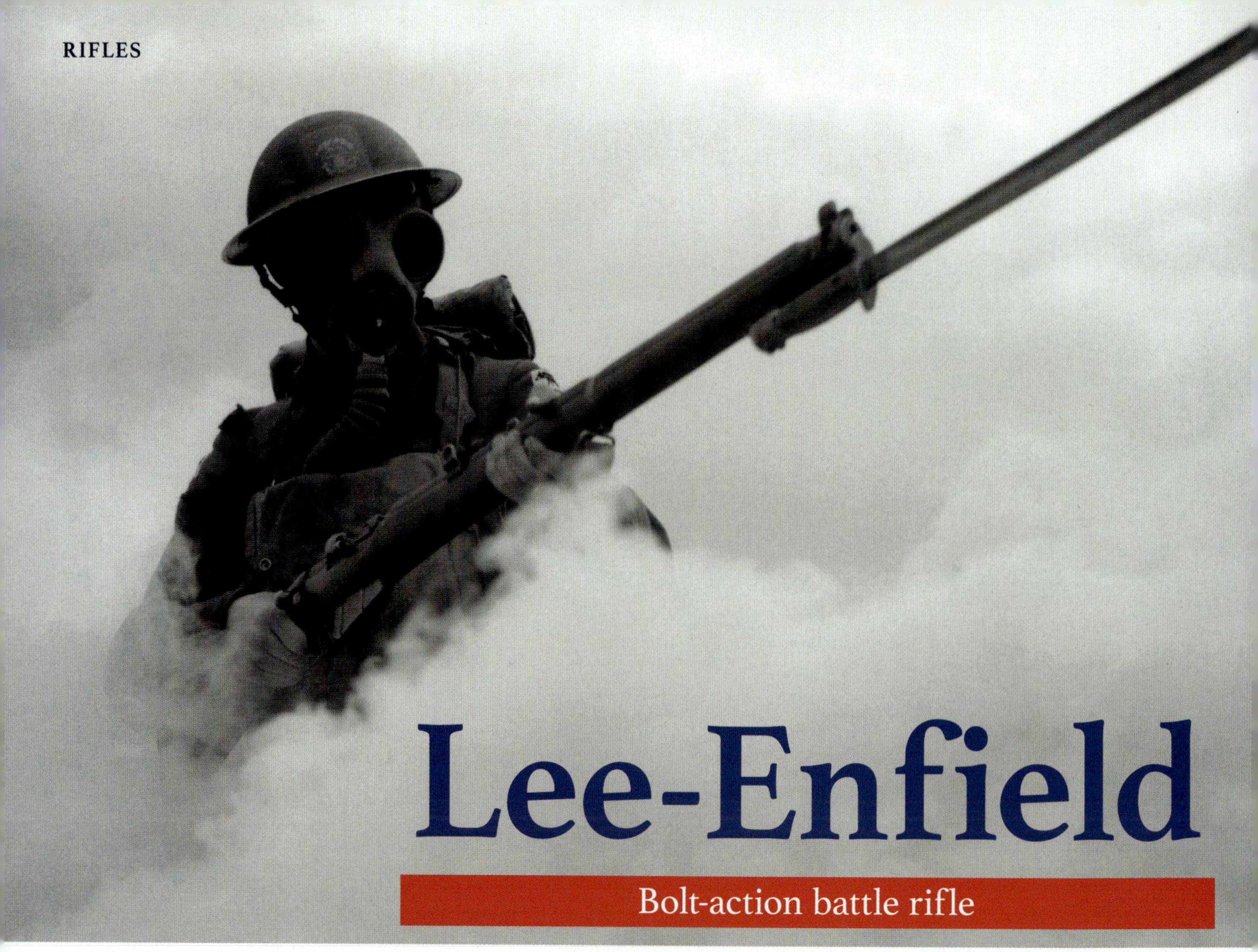

Lee-Enfield

Bolt-action battle rifle

ABOVE: A posed early war image of a soldier of the 12th Battalion, Hampshire Regiment, advancing through smoke with his No 1 Mk III at the ready, while training in the UK, 1941. (IWM H10633)

RIGHT: A Canadian sniper of the Seaforth Highlanders scans for targets with his No 4 (T) rifle near Foiano, Italy, in October 1943. (LIBRARY AND ARCHIVES CANADA)

The Lee Enfield rifle stands out as the best bolt-action military rifle in history. One can argue about the Mauser having a stronger action, or the production numbers of the Mosin-Nagant M1891, but in terms of usability by an average soldier, the Lee-Enfield is by far the most practical. Its action is easily strong enough to handle its full power rifle cartridge, the famous .303 British. That action is also smooth and fast, enabling a British soldier to fire faster than his opponent with a Mauser or Arisaka. Its ten-round magazine gave the user more firepower in the first seconds of an engagement, though it had to be reloaded with five-round stripper clips. Notably, although the magazine was detachable, soldiers did not generally carry spares.

The Lee-Enfield arose from the lessons of the Boer War and its predecessor, the Lee-Metford. The rifle's name derives from that of its designer, James Lee, with that of the UK's Royal Small Arms Factory in Enfield. It served Great Britain and the Commonwealth nations as their standard rifle throughout both world wars and into the 1950s. Some 17 million Lee-Enfields of all marks left the production lines during its long service.

Two primary models of the rifle saw service during World War Two. British troops began the war with the No 1 Mark III. Standardised in 1907, this was the rifle that had seen the army through World War One; the model commonly known as the Short Magazine Lee-Enfield (SMLE). This acronym earned the rifle the nickname 'Smelly', although this was not a reflection of the British soldier's opinion of the weapon.

Lee-Enfield Rifle No. 4 Mk. I	
Calibre	.303 British
Magazine	10-round box
Length	44.4in (112.9cm)
Weight	9.13lb (4.1kg)

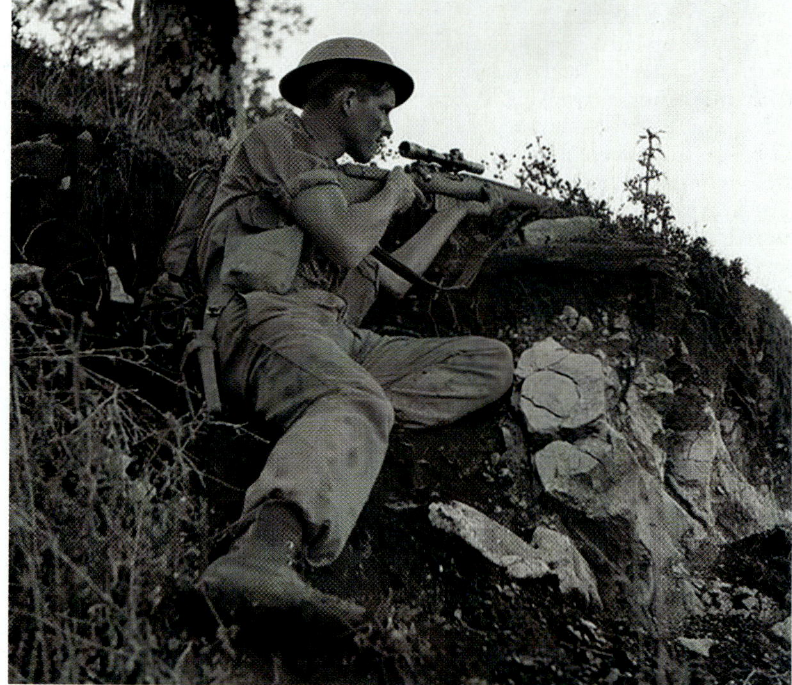

Lt Austin Mackell led Corporal John Hurst Edmondson and five privates in a counter-attack to drive them off, all of them armed with SMLEs. Despite being outnumbered and under machine gun fire, the Australians' determined assault tore into the German formation and the fighting soon became hand-to-hand. Despite suffering two wounds, Edmondson killed one German with the bayonet on his No 1 Mk. III. When Lt Mackell came under attack by three Germans, he fought so hard the stock of his own Lee-Enfield shattered. Edmondson rushed to help his officer, shooting or bayoneting all three Germans with his rifle, but sustaining further wounds. The German attack disrupted, the Australians returned to their outpost, where Edmondson died four hours later. He received a posthumous award of the Victoria Cross for his bravery, the first Australian to earn the award during World War Two.

LEFT: Indian troops from the 20th Division search for Japanese soldiers in the ruins of a train station in Burma, with SMLEs at the ready, May 1945. (IWM SE4081)

BELOW: A sergeant of No 9 Commando about to go on a patrol with his No 4 Mk I rifle at Anzio, March 1944. He carries a cloth bandolier holding extra cartridges (IWM NA12466)

As there were many rifles left over from World War One, it remained the issue weapon in 1939.

Though a high-quality weapon, a simplified version of the SMLE was needed to meet the increased demand as the UK mobilised. The No 4 Mark I boasted redesigned sights, a heavier barrel for better accuracy and the barrel protruded slightly further. The blade-type bayonet was replaced with a spike bayonet. Numbers of No 4 Mk I's began reaching field troops in mid-1942. Many soldiers preferred the older No 1 Mk III, saying it was better quality with better sights. Despite this, factories produced 4.2 million No 4s during the war.

Lee-Enfield production occurred at three plants in the UK and more abroad. Australia never adopted the No 4 and continued making the older model at the Lithgow factory. The Indian Ishapore facility did the same. No 4s were built in the UK, at the Canadian Long Branch factory and by the American firm Savage Arms. The US-built rifles had 'US Property' stamped on the receiver to justify their distribution under Lend-Lease.

Two additional models saw use during the war. The No 4 (T) equipped snipers and was considered accurate to around 600 yards. These rifles had a matched scope and were selected from the most accurate production examples, with 24,000 produced. The No 5 Mk I, popularly known as the Jungle Carbine, had a shorter barrel and a flash hider to make it handier in close terrain. It saw service in the Far East and with the UK 6th Airborne Division late in the war. The rifle had a violent recoil and muzzle blast and proved unpopular with most troops.

The Lee-Enfield rifle saw action worldwide, continuing the reputation it built during World War One. It once again proved durable and reliable in action.

An example of the expert use to which British and Commonwealth soldiers used the rifle came in April 1941. Australian troops defended Tobruk against an Axis offensive that threatened the British position in North Africa. With the Australians positioned in small strongpoints around the perimeter, during the night of April 13 a German detachment opened fire on an outpost manned by soldiers of the Australian 2-17th Infantry Battalion.

LEFT: A soldier of the 1st Battalion South Staffordshire Regiment at Mersa Matruh in October 1940. He is wearing a sand-coloured smock for camouflage. (IWM E846)

M1 Garand

ABOVE: A sergeant of the US 6th Armored Division poses with his M1. He was the first soldier of his division to set foot in Germany. (NARA)

en-bloc clip that was pushed into the rifle by the user.

After the shooter fired the last shot, the clip was automatically ejected by the rifle's mechanism. This clip made a distinctive pinging noise when it sprang from the rifle. Many stories exist of this being a disadvantage, as it announced to the enemy that one's rifle was now empty. However, there is little evidence this was an actual problem. On a noisy battlefield, with a soldier's ears already ringing from gunfire, artillery and grenade explosions, there was little chance an enemy would hear it, especially at distance. Also, soldiers are seldom alone and can be covered by a comrade while reloading.

Once in service, the M1 became the standard infantry rifle, equipping the entire rifle squad except for

Development of the M1 rifle began in the 1920s, but proceeded slowly due to the limited defence budgets of the era. The rifle gets its name from John Garand, a Canadian-born designer who worked at the US Springfield Armory. During World War Two, US troops simply called it the 'M1' or 'M1 Rifle'; the name of the designer only came into general usage later. Its very long development period allowed considerable refinement, which perhaps contributed to its great success once adopted. The US Army approved the rifle in late 1936, though production remained slow until the threat of war loomed in 1939.

By late 1941, the US Army had enough to equip most of its infantry units, but the beginning of the war dramatically increased their need. During World War Two, the Springfield Armory and Winchester produced the M1,

making more than four million. The M1 was a gas-operated semi-automatic rifle with an internal magazine loaded by an eight-shot

RIGHT: A paratrooper of the 17th Airborne Division mans an outpost near the Our River, February 1945. He has his M1 rifle and two grenades at the ready. (NARA)

those carrying the squad's Browning automatic rifle (BAR). Squad or platoon leaders might have an M1 Carbine or, rarely, a submachine gun, though many opted for the M1 rifle for its power, range and reliability. The US Marine Corps kept the older 1903 Springfield into 1942, until realising the M1's superiority. Soldiers and Marines found the rifle to be durable and easier to shoot than the old Springfield, with less recoil.

Troops who carried an M1 were almost universally positive in their praise of it. On Guadalcanal, Lt John George carried a Springfield sniper rifle. During a Japanese 'banzai charge', he was reloading when saw an American about to be bayoneted by an enemy soldier. Luckily, there were two GIs with loaded M1s nearby: "They pumped the triggers until

both clips were ringingly ejected... They lowered aim to keep the stream pouring through him as he fell to his knees, then to his haunches, then on his face, clutching his rifle tightly to the last. That Jap [sic] was alive and dangerous until perhaps the last two rounds were fired."

One US Army ordnance officer later wrote of the rifle's durability. A soldier turned in a rifle collected from a battlefield, rusted shut and covered in mud, apparently for months. Thinking it ruined, the officer believed it still

M1 Garand	
Calibre	.30
Capacity	8-round clip
Length	43.6in (110.7cm)
Weight	9.5lb (4.31kg)

had a live round in the chamber, so he held it at arm's length toward enemy lines and squeezed the trigger, hoping to at least clear it for his troops to dispose of it. The M1 fired perfectly, even cycling properly and loading the next round in the clip. He turned it in for cleaning and re-issue.

In the Pacific, it took time for the US Marines to be completely equipped with the M1, since they had adopted it late. One Marine, armed with a Springfield, followed a sergeant armed with an M1 on a patrol, staying so close the sergeant finally asked him what he was doing. The Marine said he was waiting for the sergeant to get hit, saying: "You'll probably get yours on the first burst, Mac. Before you hit the ground, I'll throw this damn Springfield away and grab your rifle!"

A sniper version, the M1C, came into service shortly before the war ended. A launcher attachment made it possible to fire rifle grenades, using special blank cartridges. Otherwise, the rifle saw little modification during the war. Some were supplied to the UK through Lend-Lease but saw limited use. About half were later returned to the United States and sold to civilian collectors.

The M1's impact proved tremendous. US Infantry had a distinct firepower advantage over enemy riflemen, who were armed with bolt-action rifles with five-round capacity. Both Germany and Japan attempted to get their own semi-automatic design into service during the war, partly due to the effectiveness of the M1. Use of semi and fully automatic weapons proliferated during the war, as the Garand proved they were easier to use and maintain than the bolt-action types.

ABOVE: A medic tends to a wounded captain, while in the background a soldier lays down covering fire with his M1 in a French town, September 1944. (NARA)

ABOVE LEFT: A rifleman uses a destroyed German infantry gun as cover while firing at a sniper in Aachen, October 1944. (NARA)

LEFT: A GI grabs a bandolier of ammunition for his M1 as he passes a British Churchill tank during an offensive near Münster, Germany, in April 1945. Each bandolier held six eight-round clips for the rifle. (NARA)

M1 Carbine

Secondary weapon won battlefield pedigree

ABOVE: A military policeman with a slung carbine directing traffic. The weapon was designed as a lightweight arm for troops such as these. (NARA)

BELOW RIGHT: Chindit leaders after the capture of Mogaung in then-Burma. At right, Major James Lumley cradles his M1 Carbine. Chindit leader 'Mad' Mike Calvert is to the right with a slung SMLE. (IWM MH7287)

BELOW: A soldier demonstrates the M3 Carbine with infrared night-vision scope. Though short-ranged, the weapon inflicted disproportionately heavy casualties on the Japanese at Okinawa. (NARA)

The US Army adopted the M1 Carbine as a replacement for the pistol and submachine gun for issue to rear echelon troops. Its sound design and utility caused Allied troops to use it as a primary battlefield weapon in all theatres. During the war, ten separate companies manufactured it and more than six million were produced, two million more than the primary US rifle, the M1 Garand.

In 1938, the US Army Infantry Board put out a requirement for a 'light rifle'. It wanted something weighing about 5lbs with an effective range of 300 yards. This new lightweight weapon would be issued to officers, ammunition carriers, men assigned to crew served weapons such as machine guns, mortars and artillery, and rear echelon troops who only needed weapons for defence against commandos and paratroopers. This would give them a more effective and longer-ranged weapon than a pistol.

After testing, a prototype from the Winchester Corporation was selected as the clear winner. Contracts were issued in late 1941, just before the United States entered the war. The sudden increase in demand led to more companies manufacturing the new carbine.

In service, the carbine quickly proved itself. Troops who would otherwise have only had a pistol appreciated its greater range and firepower. Its light weight and handiness made it easy to use and carry. A pouch for two spare magazines could be worn on the soldier's web belt or slipped onto the carbine's stock, allowing it to be carried with extra ammunition at hand. This helped soldiers such as artillery crewmen, who often did not wear kit when servicing their guns. Soldiers generally referred to the weapon as the 'carbine', while calling the larger M1 Garand the 'M1' or 'M1 Rifle'.

A few complaints arose about the carbine's relatively low-powered cartridge and lack of range and accuracy beyond 300 yards.

However, such criticisms compare the carbine with the M1 Garand rifle, which it was never intended to replace. When compared with the M1911 pistol or submachine guns, the weapon measures up favourably. A few critics stated the .45-calibre cartridge used in the M1911 or Thompson had better stopping power due to its heavier bullet, but opinions vary. The .30 Carbine round was superior to the .45 cartridge at penetrating steel helmets or light cover. Critically, .30 Carbine ammunition had the advantage of being produced with non-corrosive primers, which made the weapon much easier to keep clean.

During the war, the US Army developed the M1A1 version with a folding stock for paratroopers. Eventually, the army issued a small bag paratroopers could attach to their kit that contained the weapon with its stock folded. Prior to that, paratroopers would often tuck it behind the reserve parachute worn on the front of the chest and stomach. However, during jumps the weapon would often shift and strike the soldier in the jaw.

The M2 Carbine appeared in the last months of the war and saw limited service before the conflict ended. It had fully automatic capability and used a 30-round magazine, which later became common issue for all carbines. The M3 Carbine used a novel infrared night-vision scope to provide night-fighting capability. The scope system had a large, heavy battery the soldier had to carry with the rifle, but it did give night-vision capability out to about 70 yards. A few saw use on Okinawa where they proved valuable against night-time infiltration tactics used by the Japanese. One report stated that during the first seven days of the fighting, M3 Carbines accounted for 30 per cent of Japanese casualties inflicted by small arms fire.

John George served as an infantry officer on Guadalcanal and later with Merrill's Marauders jungle warfare unit in Burma. He was also a competitive rifle shooter with extensive firearms experience. His observations on the weapon are notable. At first on Guadalcanal, carbines were unavailable, but once they arrived, George found them very useful in the jungle environment, though the protruding magazine sometimes got caught on foliage.

George stated his preference for the carbine in the jungle, carrying four spare magazines in his pockets. Later, on the Lido Road he attacked a Japanese machine gun position, killing "...seven Japanese, spread compactly on the grass... a testimony to the effectiveness of the .30-calibre M1 carbine". He also found it easier to train new soldiers on the carbine, as opposed to the pistol.

British and French troops also used the carbine extensively, particularly among British special operations forces such as the SAS and Chindits. After the war, the US military used it through the 1960s and it was widely distributed to allies as military aid. Police forces worldwide used them, too, and they still appear in armouries as a reserve weapon. A few experts consider it an early assault rifle, due to its size and use of an intermediate cartridge, though it was not designed as such.

M1/M2 Carbine	
Calibre	.30 Carbine
Magazine	15 or 30-round box
Length	35.6in (90.4cm)
Weight	5.2lb (2.36kg)
Rate of Fire	750 rpm (M2 only)

LEFT: A classic image of a US Marine on Guam with his M1 Carbine at the ready. Note how he has taped his dogtags to reduce noise and reflection, though he still wears a ring on his hand. (USMC)

BELOW: US Marines on Tinian firing at Japanese troops during the mop-up phase. Two have carbines while the rest have M1 rifles. (USMC)

M1903 Springfield

The M1903 Springfield rifle saw extensive service in World War Two despite being replaced by the M1 Garand as the primary infantry rifle. Adopted in 1903, the rifle served in the US conflict in the Philippines, World War One and the various American military involvements in the western hemisphere and elsewhere between the wars. Along the way it developed a solid reputation as a dependable, accurate and sturdy rifle, equal to the German Mauser 98.

Unfortunately, the M1903 proved a little too similar to the Mauser, leading to patent infringement lawsuits against the US government for the rifle, the stripper clip used to load it, and the design of the bullet used in its ammunition. The various cases were not resolved until 1928, by which time the US government paid an extra $612,000 for the privilege of making the M1903.

By the time the US entered World War Two, the M1903 had been replaced as the primary infantry rifle by the M1 in the US Army, but the US Marine Corps retained the M1903, hesitant to accept the new semi-automatic. Marine leadership quickly changed their minds once combat proved the M1 superior, but the Marines carried the Springfield during its initial campaigns at Guadalcanal and elsewhere. Army

troops already in the Philippines when the war began were also equipped with M1903s. US troops usually called the rifle the '03' or the Springfield.

Initially, the M1 could not fire rifle grenades, so many infantry squads still had an M1903 for that purpose. Rear-echelon troops were also issued M1903s to free up more modern weapons for the frontline units. It also served effectively as a sniper rifle in all theatres. The Springfield stayed in production for much of the war and was liberally distributed to Free French Forces in North Africa, the Brazilian Expeditionary Force and Chinese troops.

The US Marines used the M1903 longer for frontline combat until enough M1s were available. While Marines prized good marksmanship, they also understood that most of the firepower in a company came from its machine guns and BARs (Browning automatic rifles). Springfield-equipped riflemen were vital in guarding the flanks of the automatic weapons teams and giving supporting fire. This combination of accurate rifle fire and the heavy firepower of the automatic weapons enabled Marine units to inflict heavy casualties during Japanese attacks, particularly when Japanese leaders sent their troops forward in bayonet attacks or 'banzai' charges.

Springfield M1903	
Calibre	.30
Magazine	5-round internal
Length	43.5in (110.5cm)
Weight	9lb (4.1kg)

MAS36

The last bolt-action rifle

250,000 were available when the war began. After France fell in mid-1940, the German military took over large numbers of them and issued them to troops garrisoned in France, which eased supply of ammunition. Outside France, the weapon continued to serve in Vichy and some Free French units, including the Foreign Legion. These saw action against Axis forces in North Africa.

However, with France occupied for much of the war, ammunition and parts were an issue. From 1943, Free French Forces were rearmed with British and American small arms, including the MAS36's equivalent, the M1903 Springfield, often seen in photographs. This effectively ended widespread use of the MAS36 for the rest of the war.

After the war, France put the MAS36 back into production, using it until the early 1960s. Eventually, the MAS factory turned out more than a million rifles, and they often turn up in areas where France held influence.

LEFT: These Free Polish troops are in France in 1940. They have been issued French equipment and are carrying MAS36 rifles. (POLISH NATIONAL ARCHIVES)

BELOW: French Foreign Legion troops advance toward an enemy position at the Battle of Bir Hakeim, June 1942. The spike bayonets are extended on their MAS36 rifles. (IWM E13313)

Fusil MAS36	
Calibre	7.5mm
Magazine	5-round internal box
Length	40.1in (101.9cmcm)
Weight	8.1lbs (3.67kg)

In the mid-1930s, France adopted a new rifle to replace the millions of older Lebel and Berthier rifles in its inventory. This new weapon, the MAS36, is notably the last bolt-action infantry rifle designed for a military force; everything since has been semi and/or fully automatic. It fired a new 7.5mm cartridge designed and tested in the 1920s. Like many other weapons designs between the world wars, its development was delayed due to restrictive budgets and the low perceived need for a new weapon when there were large numbers of surplus World War One small arms in storage.

The MAS acronym stands for Manufacture d'Armes de Saint-Étienne, one of the major French arsenals of the period. Despite being designed in the mid-1930s, it is a simple bolt-action rifle similar to weapons made decades earlier. Its most notable features are the lack of a safety mechanism and a distinct forward curve to the bolt handle. The rifle's spike bayonet, which was stored in a tube beneath the barrel, was simply removed, flipped in the opposite direction and clipped back into the rifle. Although a rather dated design, the weapon performed well, being of quality manufacture and reliable in use.

Production proceeded slowly until the war started so that only about

Tokarev Rifles

Like the United States, the Soviet Union put considerable effort into developing a semi-automatic rifle for infantry use. Work began in the early 1930s with working rifles entering service in time for the Winter War with Finland and the fighting against Japan in the Far East. The first model, designed by Sergei Simonov, received the designation AVS36. It performed poorly and was withdrawn from service, only to reappear in the desperate early days of the German invasion when any weapon was issued to the troops.

Another design, from weapons designer Fedor Tokarev, saw limited success. The SVT38 entered production in 1939 and also saw use during the Winter War. However, combat revealed its mechanism, while solid in design, was too delicate for field use and the rifle was also considered a failure. Since around 150,000 SVT38s came off the production lines before cancellation, the rifle also saw use in the early period of the war.

An improved version, the SVT40, entered service in 1940 and was more successful, although Soviet troops continued to report problems with it similar to the SVT38. One complaint mentioned its severe muzzle blast, so a muzzle brake was fitted to reduce it. The Red Army wanted a semi-automatic rifle to replace the bolt-action Mosin Nagant M1891/30, but once the war with Germany began in June 1941, production could not keep pace with demand. The M1891/30 remained the primary rifle, with SVT40s often issued piecemeal, a few to a unit. Unit leaders often gave the few SVT40s to reliable non-commissioned officers or capable soldiers considered able to make best use of the rifle.

A sniper version with a telescopic sight also saw wide use and was issued to sharpshooters. Thousands of these rifles fell into German and Finnish hands and were turned against their original owners. The Germans in particular suffered from a lack of semi-automatic rifles and used the SVT40 extensively. Its design influenced the German Gewehr 43. The Soviets built around 1.5 million SVT40s, not enough to replace the M1891/30. About 50,000 were sniper versions.

RIGHT: An Estonian volunteer in the Finnish Army uses an SVT40 rifle in June 1944. (SA-KUVA)

BELOW: Two Soviet soldiers advance, bayonets affixed to their SVT40 rifles. The rifle was never widely issued but some units received larger numbers of them. (RIAN 613474)

Tokarev SVT40	
Calibre	7.62mmx54R
Magazine	10-round box
Length	48.1in (122.2cm)
Weight	8.58lb (3.89kg)

Mosin-Nagant M1891/30

Long-serving Russian/Soviet infantry rifle

The Mosin-Nagant M1891 rifle is often dismissed as a crude, primitive rifle, far below the qualitative standards of its peers, such as the SMLE, Mauser 98K and M1903 Springfield. However, its relative simplicity and rough finish conceal a rifle that is sturdy, reliable and able to be used and maintained by conscripts with limited training. This made it a good weapon for the Red Army. The M1891 began service in the 1890s under Imperial Russia and examples have been seen at time of writing in the Russia-Ukraine war, giving the rifle a service life of 134 years and counting.

The standard model in production during World War Two was the M1891/30, although older models were certainly pressed into service. The major changes included a slightly shortened barrel (though still long at 79cm), recalibration of the sight to metres instead of the archaic Russian unit of measurement called the arshin, and some machining changes to speed manufacture. A shorter-barrelled carbine called the M1938 was also issued to artillery troops, military police and rear-echelon troops.

Finland produced its own versions of the M1891. It inherited thousands of them when it became independent after World War One, so it made sense to use what was available. The Finns also captured thousands more during the Winter War.

Mosin-Nagant M1891/30	
Calibre	7.62x54R
Magazine	5-round internal box
Length	48.5in (123.2cm)
Weight	8.8lbs (4kg)
Action	Bolt-action

The biggest problem the Red Army experienced with the M1891 was the constant shortage of them, particularly early in the war. Often, soldiers were not issued a rifle and ammunition until they were beginning an operation, with little time for training. Film scenes of soldiers going into battle unarmed and having to pick up a weapon from a fallen comrade are not entirely false. However, the rifle was well liked and trusted by soldiers when they had them. One reason the Red Army used submachine guns so extensively was to make up for shortages of rifles.

Even so, production of the M1891/30 exceeded 13 million from 1930 to 1943, with more produced in the final two years of the war. Such high numbers reveal the incredible losses of weapons and equipment during the conflict as well as the need to arm the massive Red Army.

M1891 rifles saw wide use as sniper rifles. Soviet snipers preferred them over most other models. Snipers such as Vasily Zaitsev (242 kills) and Lyudmilla Pavlichenko (309 kills) used these weapons to great effect. Pavlichenko even had her image used on a Soviet postage stamp in her honour.

ABOVE: Finnish soldiers man a trench with their M1891 rifles. The Finns valued marksmanship and could generally outshoot their poorly trained Soviet counterparts. (SA-KUVA)

LEFT: Soviet infantry squads were often armed with a variety of weapons. Here, a rifleman advances past a light machine gunner and two submachine gunners in Krymskaya in May 1943. (RUSSIAN ARCHIVES)

Arisaka Rifles

Japan's version of the Mauser

The Japanese Empire used two major types of rifles during the war. They were heavily influenced by Mauser designs of the late 1800s and are generally known by the name Arisaka, after Arisaka Nariakira, a Japanese army officer and weapons designer.

Type 38: Adopted in 1905, the Type 38 used the 6.5mm cartridge, a lighter cartridge more suited to the smaller stature of Japanese soldiers at the time. It also used a simplified bolt for easier cleaning, a dust cover based on experience from the Russo-Japanese War of 1904-05, and gas escape holes to channel gases away from the firer in case a cartridge case ruptured in the chamber. Japan built the Type 38 in three factories in Japan and two in occupied Korea and China, producing more than 3.5 million before manufacture ended in 1944. Though less powerful, the 6.5mm cartridge also produced less smoke

and muzzle flash, allowing Japanese troops to remain hidden more easily in forest and jungle terrain.

Type 99: In the late 1930s, the Japanese decided to adopt a larger, more powerful rifle cartridge, the 7.7mm. To accommodate the new round, the Type 38 was modified as the Type 99. This design incorporated a wire monopod to aid in accurate shooting, and a chrome plated bore and bolt face to reduce corrosion. The Type 99 entered production in 1941 and 2.5 million were built before the war ended. Late production models were increasingly crude due to manufacturing and material problems; some late-war rifles were actually dangerous to fire.

All Arisaka rifles bore a chrysanthemum symbol on the receiver. This marked the rifle as the property of the emperor, charging the soldier it was issued to with its care and maintenance. When the rifles had to be surrendered at the end of the war, these marking were generally ground off or defaced. An Arisaka with an intact chrysanthemum is a rare collector's item today.

In line with Japan's military ethos of the time, Arisakas were issued with long bayonets. Japanese tactical doctrine placed considerable importance on closing with the enemy to finish them with the bayonet. Even those not issued a rifle would have a bayonet. New recruits in China would be 'blooded' by ordering them to bayonet a Chinese prisoner. On the World War Two battlefield – among the artillery, machine guns and naval gunfire – closing with the bayonet proved difficult and often failed to accomplish anything but heavy losses for the Japanese force.

Arisaka Rifles		
	Type 38	Type 99
Calibre	6.5mm	7.7mm
Magazine	5-round internal	5-round internal
Length	50.2in (127.5cm)	44in (111.8cm)
Weight	9.25lb (4.2kg)	8.4lb (3.8kg)

Carcano Rifles

Italy's forgotten rifles

Like the Japanese Arisaka, the Italian name Carcano refers to a series of Italy's military rifles made from the late 1800s through to the end of World War Two. Initial models came from the Turin Army Arsenal, designed by Salvatore Carcano, an army veteran who worked at the arsenal after completing his service. This first entered service in 1891 and naturally received the designation Model 1891, often shortened to Model 91 or M91. Various versions of this 6.5mm rifle equipped Italian troops through both world wars.

This rifle is often misnamed the 'Mannlicher-Carcano', but Austrian weapons designer Ferdinand von Mannlicher only invented the en-bloc clip system used on the Carcano, similar to that used on the M1 Garand. On the Carcano, this clip held six rounds as loaded into the rifle and when the last shot was fired the clip fell from a slot in the bottom of the magazine. The rifle uses a Mauser-type action and in Italy was known as the 'Mauser-Parravicino', after Gen Gustavo Parravicino, once head of the Italian Infantry Shooting School who recommended the rifle for service. Italian soldiers just called it the '91'.

Several versions of the M91 saw service during the war. The M91/38 carbine and M91/41 rifle were the most modern. The Italian military attempted to upgrade its rifle calibre to a larger 7.35mm round in the late 1930s, but this effort stalled when the war began, and Italian forces reverted to the 6.5mm as there was no time to convert the entire military to the newer cartridge.

Many complaints arose about the 6.5mm's poor performance. It was considered weak compared with other rifle cartridges and there was evidence of different lot numbers and even types of gunpowder being mixed in ammunition production, badly affecting accuracy and performance in action. A saying existed, calling the Carcano "the rifle that never gets angry because it has never intentionally hurt anybody". In reality, properly made 6.5mm ammunition proved accurate and usable, if a bit underpowered.

After Italy withdrew from the war, German units quickly disarmed Italian army units, acquiring thousands of Carcano rifles. Many of these were later issued to Volkssturm militia units in the last days of the war. The Carcano also saw wide use among partisans in Yugoslavia.

Carcano M91/38	
Calibre	6.5mm
Magazine	6-round en-bloc clip
Length	40.1in (101.8cm)
Weight	7.5lb (3.4kg)

ABOVE: An Italian partisan in Florence, Italy, in August 1944. Note his cartridge belt, loaded with six-round clips. After the last shot was fired, the clip fell out of the slot in the bottom of the rifle's magazine. (IWM TR2282)

LEFT: After Italy withdrew from the war, Germany confiscated many Carcano rifles. Many were later used by Volkssturm militia in the last-ditch defence of Germany, as with these militia near Konigsberg in January 1945. (BUNDESARCHIV BILD 183-R98401)

Mauser 98

The standard for bolt-action rifles

ABOVE: A German sniper and his spotter in the Soviet Union, June 1942. (BUNDESARCHIV BILD 101I-216-0417-19)

The Mauser Model 1898 is the most widely used bolt-action military rifle in history and served as the German military's standard issue rifle. Many other nations produced this design, some under licence and some using machinery received as war reparations. Mausers of different patterns saw use by many of the combatant nations including Poland, Yugoslavia and China. The rifle's popularity in China turned the name Mauser into a synonym for rifle in that nation. Several other weapons borrowed or directly copied from the Model 1898, including the Japanese Arisaka and the US Springfield M1903.

This makes the Mauser design the most widely used type by far. For World War Two, the Germans standardised on the Mauser 98K, with the letter K standing for Kurz, or short. The original Mauser rifles used in World War One had longer barrels, so the Germans classified their new version as a carbine; officially the 98K was the Karabiner 98K. However, the 98K was roughly the same size as many service rifles of the period, such as the US M1903 or the UK's SMLE. As with many widely used weapons, several names are in use for it, including Kar98K, Mauser 98, 98K and simply the Mauser.

The 98K entered production in 1935 and was still being made when the war ended. German factories turned out roughly 12-14 million 98Ks from 1935-45, with the true number still a matter of argument among those interested. Not surprisingly, during the war manufacturing quality fell sharply due to material shortages and other problems.

Older Mausers saw use in Germany during the war, but not in frontline service until the desperate last days. They could be found mixed in with the foreign weapons used by the Volkssturm near the end of the war, but the 98K armed the Wehrmacht as a primary weapon throughout

RIGHT: A soldier aims his rifle during the Warsaw Uprising in 1944. He has another 98K slung on his back, perhaps taken from a wounded comrade or recovered from a dead or captured partisan. (BUNDESARCHIV BILD 101I-695-0403-30)

Mauser 98K	
Calibre	7.92mm
Magazine	5-round internal
Length	43.6in (110.8cm)
Weight	8.6lb (3.9kg)

LEFT: These Volkssturm militia troops are lucky to have received Mausers rather than a captured weapon or poorly made Volkssturm rifle. Some of these older men may have used the Mauser in World War One. (BUNDESARCHIV_BILD_146-1979-107-14)

a handful of grenades shattered the Soviet formation and drove them back. An hour later, the Germans managed to get a fresh supply of ammunition through to the defenders.

In other situations, the 98K proved inadequate. Gottlieb Biderman served on the Eastern Front and recalled appropriating a Soviet PPSh-41 submachine gun as soon as he could: "I took one of the submachine guns and several drum magazines from one of the prisoners for my own use, as I no longer placed much faith in the slow-firing 98K carbine for close combat. I felt more confident equipped with the high-capacity automatic weapon, and it was to remain with me for many months."

After the war, millions of 98Ks were taken by the victorious Allies and distributed as military aid, allowing the rifle to spread across the world. The Soviets distributed them to communist movements in Vietnam and elsewhere. Others were destroyed or taken over by formerly occupied nations as they rebuilt their militaries. Many are in the hands of civilian collectors, who converse endlessly about proof marks and production numbers.

BELOW: A soldier takes aim with his 98K in southern Russia, April 1943. He may be shooting at a distant target, as his fellow soldier is standing in the open. (POLISH NATIONAL ARCHIVES)

the war. When Germany occupied nations like Czechoslovakia and Belgium, where Mauser derivatives were made, they simply took over the factories and continued production.

When World War Two began, the Mauser was actually becoming obsolete, particularly against semi-automatic designs such as the US M1 and Soviet Tokarev SVT40. However, most nations still used bolt-action service rifles, most of them dated to World War One or even earlier. This made the Mauser competitive and, once the war began, Germany had no choice but to keep the weapon in service, as it could not make its own more advanced designs in sufficient numbers.

In service, the Mauser in whatever version proved sturdy and dependable, easily able to handle full-powered rifle cartridges. It stood up well against harsh conditions from the steppes of Russia to the North African desert as long as it got anything approaching reasonable maintenance. The rifle's accuracy

proved good enough for field use and sniper versions of the 98K were deadly to Allied troops. One member of the American 1st Special Service Force used a Mauser sniper rifle he captured, recalling: "That thing was so deadly. It was a little heavy, but boy, you just put the crosshairs on anything, and it was done for."

German infantry squads centred around their machine gun, with the riflemen carrying ammunition and protecting it. The machine gun provided most of the squad's firepower. However, well-aimed rifle fire could be decisive, too. In November 1942, Soviet troops encircled the German occupied village of Verkhne-Golubaya in the Stalingrad perimeter. After a time, the Germans ran low on ammunition, with only eight to ten rounds per rifleman. A Soviet infantry attack loomed, with the Red Army troops approaching in a close formation. A detachment of German riflemen crept forward to meet them and opened fire when the Soviets were only 20 yards away. Just a few rifle shots and

FG42

Germany's innovative paratrooper rifle

ABOVE: A German paratrooper poses with his FG42 rifle. This appears to be a propaganda image as the rifle's sights are folded down in the storage position. (BUNDESARCHIV BILD 101I-720-0344-11)

The design channelled recoil straight back into the shooter's shoulder to limit muzzle rise and the sights could be folded down to protect them. It extensively used metal stampings as with other wartime designs.

The rifle entered service in early 1944 and proved popular with German airborne troops. There were several production variants, with most of the differences being simplifications to accelerate manufacture. Despite its innovative features, only about 7,000 were made and its influence on the battlefield was negligible. The FG42 became far more influential in post-war weapons design.

The FG42's firepower could be fearsome in action. A US Army Paratrooper sergeant wrote about the weapon's potential after an ambush near the Rhine River in March 1945. His squad, moving along the riverbank, suddenly took what they thought was machine gun fire. Three men were hit by the first burst before a second burst killed their lieutenant. The sergeant saw one of the Germans rise to fire and realised the enemy did not have a machine gun. "He had one of the dreaded FG42s in his possession... a third FG42 opened up from a wooded area... hitting five men. Before we could reposition, manoeuvre and counter-attack, the Germans had successfully retreated, not being held up by the weight of a larger machine gun. Our squad took eight casualties while seeing only one German."

The FG42 arose from a Luftwaffe requirement for a new rifle for airborne troops (unlike other armies, Germany's airborne forces fell under its air force). Limitations in German parachute design meant soldiers jumped with only a pistol and hand grenades. Their heavier weapons were stored in a drop container the paratroopers had to access after landing. This naturally put them at a disadvantage if they had to engage their enemy on landing. The requirements specified a weapon that was compact, relatively lightweight and had good firepower. The letters FG stand for Fallschirmjägergewehr or 'paratrooper rifle'.

The resulting FG42 incorporated several innovative features, though it fired the standard full-power 7.92mm rifle cartridge. It used a side-mounted ten or 20-round magazine that lowered the rifle's profile and shortened it since the magazine group could be placed directly above the trigger group in the receiver. A bipod attached under the barrel aided in stable shooting. The FG42 fired semi-automatically from a closed bolt or fully-automatically from an open bolt to delay overheating.

RIGHT: A German paratrooper with an FG42 poses near a glider during the Gran Sasso mission to rescue Benito Mussolini. Famed German commando Otto Skorzeny planned and launched the successful raid. (BUNDESARCHIV BILD 101I-567-1503A-01)

FG42	
Calibre	7.92x57mm
Magazine	10/20-round box
Length	37in (94cm)
Weight	10lb (4.53kg)
Rate of Fire	750-900 rpm

Gewehr 43

When Germany invaded the Soviet Union in June 1941, they quickly ran into the wide range of small arms the Red Army issued, including the Tokarev semi-automatic rifles. These surprised the Germans, who were only beginning to experiment with such designs. Germany's first production semi-automatic rifle was the Gewehr 41, which fired the same cartridge as the Mauser 98K, but used a non-detachable ten-round magazine. Two versions were made, one by Mauser, which performed poorly, and another by Walther, whose simplified version proved better in service. The two companies built about 120,000 before production shifted to the Gewehr 43 (G43).

The G43 combined experience from the G41 and from captured Tokarevs. It also chambered the standard 7.92mm round, but used a detachable ten-round magazine for faster reloading. The G43's design directly copied the Tokarev's gas system. In 1944, the Wehrmacht changed the name of the Gewehr 43 to Karabiner (carbine) 43 and made the rifle 50mm shorter. Otherwise, the K43 was identical. Wartime production quality never matched that of other semi-automatics like the M1 Garand, but about 400,000 were made before the war ended. More than 53,000 rifles were completed as sniper rifles with the ZF-4 scope.

There were never enough G43s to equip entire units, and the rifle was usually seen mixed in with Mausers and StG44s. The sniper version was not as accurate as a Mauser sniper rifle, but at typical battlefield combat ranges it was effective.

Former soldier Sepp Allerberger recalled using one at close range during a Soviet attack: "I began firing round after round of accurate fire over open sights at a range of about 80 metres. To be sure of the hit, and for the explosive round to do its work, I aimed for the area just above the hip... The magazine of my semi-automatic held ten rounds. Once the first clip was empty, every shot hit, I swiftly fitted the second and continued firing." The reference to explosive bullets referred to the German use of exploding 'observation cartridges', usually used in aircraft to correct fire in the air. Soviet snipers often used similar ammunition.

Sniper Franz Kramer also used explosive bullets in his G43. In one battle, he used them to shoot down

LEFT: A German unit stops to rest on the Eastern Front, 1944. The seated soldier cradles a Gewehr 43 while his comrade has a StG44. (BUNDESARCHIV BILD 1011-090-3912-19A)

Gewehr 43	
Calibre	7.92x57mm
Magazine	10-round box
Length	44in (111.7cm)
Weight	9.7lb (4.4kg)

advancing Russians, starting with those in the rear of the group. After hitting ten Soviets, the attack faltered as the screams of the Soviet wounded unnerved their comrades, causing them to withdraw. Such actions highlight the brutality of the fighting on the Eastern Front.

LEFT: A German soldier takes aim with his G43 on the Eastern Front. The elevation on his rear sight indicates he is shooting at a distant target. (BUNDESARCHIV)

Sturmgewehr 44

ABOVE: A German soldier in a camouflage cap and smock holds his StG44 in July 1944. Note the pouch for three magazines on his belt. (BUNDESARCHIV BILD 101I-676-7996-13)

ABOVE RIGHT: German grenadiers attempt to fight their way out of a forest after becoming trapped there during the Ardennes Offensive on December 22, 1944. The nearest man has an StG44. (BUNDESARCHIV BILD 183-1985-0104-501)

RIGHT: This soldier has a ZF-4 scope attached to his MP43/1 in 1943. Firing in full-automatic tended to ruin the sight's zero. (BUNDESARCHIV BILD 146-1979-118-55)

The Sturmgewehr 44 (StG44) made history as the world's first practical assault rifle. The weapon evolved through several developmental versions such as the MP43/I and actually saw more combat service than is widely known. It is often referred to by its interim name, the MP44. Here we use its final name of Sturmgewehr ('assault rifle').

Design of this revolutionary new weapon actually began in the early 1920s, as the German army absorbed the lessons of World War One and the new restrictions of the Versailles Treaty, which placed hard limits on the size and armament of the military. The current full-power rifle cartridges, such as the 7.92mm round in the Mauser, were powerful and had an effective range much farther than the average soldier could reasonably shoot. Their weight and size also limited how much ammunition could be carried.

Discussion centred around an intermediate cartridge, more powerful than a pistol round but weaker than a rifle round, though still effective out to 400 metres. Such a round would fit into a detachable magazine of 20-30 rounds capacity and be more controllable in fully automatic fire. Research proceeded slowly until the 1930s, when work accelerated, but the military had little interest until after the war began, when German troops encountered the large number of automatic weapons used by the Soviets. By then an intermediate cartridge existed, the 7.92x33mm Kurz, or 'short.'

By November 1942 a prototype, the MKb42 (H), entered production, but fewer than 12,000 were made. The military soon renamed it the MP43 – for machinenpistole, or submachine gun, possibly to disguise it from Hitler, who disapproved of the concept. Eventually, a German War Ministry technician overcame Hitler's resistance, and the MP43 went into full production. In April 1944, the name changed to MP44, and finally in December 1944, Hitler personally assigned the name Sturmgewehr 44, likely part of his penchant for giving weapons aggressive sounding names as the war became more desperate.

Despite the somewhat convoluted development history, the StG44 proved very practical in field use. Its weight compared favourably with standard rifles of the day, particularly considering its 30-round magazine. It fired from a closed bolt for better accuracy, proved simple to use and maintain, and was controllable in automatic fire. Field use revealed it was best to fire the StG44 in semi-automatic for better controllability and the magazine springs proved weak, so that only 25 rounds were loaded. Other quality control problems plagued the weapon, often in the last year of the war, when such problems became common to all German weapons as production faltered under the strain of looming defeat.

The rifle was issued with pouches for three spare magazines; a soldier

Sturmgewehr 44	
Calibre	7.92x33mm Kurz
Magazine	30-round box
Length	37in (94cm)
Weight	11.5lb (5.22kg)
Rate of Fire	500 rpm

with six spare magazines had 175-210 rounds, more than a soldier with a Mauser could easily carry. The Germans designed several accessories for the rifle, including a curved barrel extension for shooting around corners. A 1.5 power scope helped with long-range accuracy, but was not suitable for true sniper use. An infrared aiming device for night shooting, similar to the one developed in the US for the M3 carbine, saw limited use on the Eastern Front in 1945. This device had a large battery pack the soldier carried on their back and was known as the 'Vampir', or Vampire.

The weapon saw issue to infantry units, though few had enough to equip more than a handful of their troops. Most photographic evidence shows StG44s alongside other German rifles and submachine guns in small numbers. By the end of the war, Germany managed to produce almost 426,000, a considerable number though not enough to replace the millions of Mausers and other arms in service.

Allied troops respected the StG44, frequently using captured examples until they ran out of ammunition. One American paratrooper, Sgt Ernest Feldman, used one on D-Day. After losing his own weapon during the parachute drop, he landed with only a pistol. At sunrise, he came across

a dead German soldier with a StG44 and four spare magazines. Fighting throughout the day, he eventually used all his ammunition, killing two German soldiers along the way. He replaced his now-useless StG44 for an M1 Garand.

After the war the East German Army and police used the StG44 until replaced by the AK47 Kalashnikov. Arguments continue as to how much the AK-series draws from the StG44, but there is no disputing the weapon's place as the first assault rifle.

ABOVE: A line of German troops during counter-attack near Aachen, December 1944. Two of them carry StG44 rifles at the ready while the lead soldier has his slung to carry a panzerfaust. (BUNDESARCHIV BILD 183-J28344)

BELOW: An American soldier carrying a captured StG44 near Château Salins, France, in November 1944. Note the German magazine pouch on his belt. (NARA)

Machine Guns

Machine guns dominated the battlefields of World War One, particularly on the Western Front. By World War Two, the proliferation of armoured vehicles and the return of mobility to warfare dampened the machine gun's primacy, but it remained an important infantry weapon. Automatic weapons became even more widely used during the conflict in various forms, with a general trend towards making them lighter and more portable.

To differentiate from the submachine gun, which fired a pistol calibre cartridge from a magazine, the machine gun served as a delivery system for full-powered rifle ammunition. Some used magazines while others used cloth or metallic belts that fed through the weapon. A few models used both. As machine guns experienced higher levels of overheating from this more powerful ammunition, they fired from an open bolt, which allowed air to circulate through them. Quick change barrels also became more common, as this

kept the weapon in action longer during sustained fighting.

During the 1930s and '40s, machine guns were usually divided into two types. Light Machine Guns (LMGs) could be carried by one person, used a bipod and were easily carried on the offensive. Some LMGs, like the US Browning Automatic Rifle (BAR),

were called automatic rifles, a nod to their limited ammunition capacity and inability to perform sustained fire. Despite being portable by a single soldier, most LMGs needed another soldier or two to carry ammunition, spare barrels and other accessories. Some nations used the term 'medium machine gun' to differentiate between two weapons in the category, such as the Browning M1919 and the BAR.

Heavy Machine Guns (HMGs) usually used the same calibres as the LMGs, but were larger, heavier and meant primarily for mounting on a tripod. Many of them used water jackets surrounding the barrel to keep the weapon cool during sustained firing. These weapons generally had a squad of five or more soldiers to move and maintain them in action. Only a few nations used HMGs in larger calibres, such as the Browning M2 .50-calibre, Soviet DShK 1938 or the Vickers .5-inch, which was really only used on vehicles.

A new type, now called the General Purpose Machine Gun (GPMG), was just entering service with the German military in the late 1930s. The MG34 began this trend toward a multipurpose machine gun, which could be used an infantry weapon, an anti-aircraft weapon, or be installed in vehicles. Its successor, the famous MG42, cemented this trend for the future; indeed, modernised versions of the MG42 are common today.

As with other weapon types, the machine guns used in World War

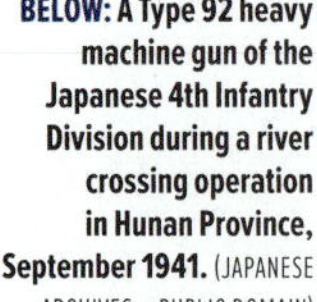

Two were a mix of new models and those left over from the previous war. Holdovers included the Vickers Mark I, Browning Model 1917 and Maxim PM1910. Generally, such holdovers stayed in service simply because there was no better replacement, and they still worked well enough in their intended role.

Joining these stalwart veterans were a host of machine guns designed during the 1920s and 30s. Some of these were excellent, such as the British Bren and MG34, while others performed poorly in field use, such as the Italian Breda Modello 30 and Japanese Type 11. The inter-war period saw extensive experimentation and not all these efforts achieved success.

Whatever type of weapon was at hand, machine guns saw wide use with infantry of every combatant nation. All developed techniques for using them offensively and defensively, but their primary role was always fire support for infantry in action.

In the attack, machine guns suppressed enemy troops so one's own infantry could manoeuvre against their objective. Depending on the army, machine guns of different types were distributed down to the squad level, or reserved to company, battalion and regimental level machine gun or heavy weapons companies. Often it was a mix of both; for example, a US Army infantry squad had a BAR in the squad with the Browning M1919 at the company level.

In the defence, machine guns could be used to man strongpoints for a unit's section of the line. At the squad level, the squad's riflemen protected the flanks of their machine gun as it provided most of the squad's firepower. Many veteran accounts mention how the Bren or BAR gunner in a squad often inflicted far more casualties in action than the rest of the squad put together.

Destroying a machine gun often meant closing with its position under fire and using grenades and small arms to kill or capture the crew. It is also notable that during the war many awards for valour, some of them posthumous, went to soldiers who attacked machine gun emplacements. When possible, infantry would call in support from armoured vehicles, artillery or air support to reduce such a position.

While no longer the stalemate-inducing weapon of 1914-1918, machine guns remained of supreme importance to infantry units. Most infantry tactics involved these weapons and their use to achieve objectives.

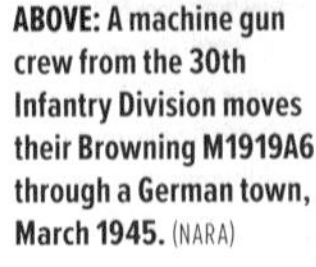

ABOVE: A machine gun crew from the 30th Infantry Division moves their Browning M1919A6 through a German town, March 1945. (NARA)

LEFT: A Finnish soldier takes aim with his Lahti M26 light machine gun. Though accurate, the weapon was complex and many Finns preferred captured Soviet weapons. (SA-KUVA)

Bren Gun

ABOVE: Two Bren gunners of D Company, 2/12th Australian Infantry Battalion fire on Japanese troops in a pillbox that has just been destroyed by the M3 Stuart tank in the background. (AWM 014001)

Among the magazine-fed light machine guns (LMGs) of the war, the Bren ranks with the best. It served as the standard section automatic weapon in the British and Commonwealth armies, providing a reliable and effective weapon. Compared with most other LMGs, the Bren was a bit heavier, but it had good magazine capacity, a quick-change barrel and high accuracy. The Bren derived in large part from the Czech ZB series of LMGs, developed in the 1920s and '30s. The name Bren is an acronym composed of the name of the Czech city of Brno, where the ZBs were designed, and Enfield, the location of the Royal Small Arms Factory in England.

When British forces withdrew from the Continent in 1940, they left behind 30,000 Brens, leaving only 2,300 in England, enough to equip just two divisions. This led to the Mk II Bren, a modified version designed to improve production. Later marks sought to reduce weight, but all versions of the Bren were functionally similar. The parts were interchangeable and, as with most military weapons, parts from different marks were often mixed together during maintenance and rebuilding.

Factories in the UK, Canada, Australia and India produced about

RIGHT: Two Kachin Rangers operate a Bren in a blocking position in Burma, ready to fire on retreating Japanese troops. (NARA)

a half million Brens during the war. In Canada, the weapons were made at the Inglis factory. There a female worker, Veronica Foster, gained fame as 'Ronnie, the Bren Gun Girl', a predecessor to the fictional 'Rosie the Riveter' in the United States.

The British infantry section contained a seven-soldier rifle group and a three-man Bren group with a No 1 gunner and No 2 assistant gunner who carried extra ammunition, the spare barrel and cleaning tools. The group leader, usually a lance corporal, also carried additional magazines. This gave an infantry platoon three Brens for fire support. To keep the gun in action, all members of a platoon carried extra magazines. The assistant gunner had a special pouch used to collect magazines from the rest of the section. In practice, Bren teams used these first and saved their own magazines for emergencies. As with other LMGs, skilled Bren gunners were often able to inflict more casualties on their enemy than the rest of the platoon combined.

Each infantry battalion also had a platoon of 13 Universal Carriers, small, tracked vehicles used for transport or scouting. Each carried a Bren, leading to the vehicle often being referred to as a Bren Carrier. Brens also saw use in the anti-aircraft role, equipped with a suitable mount and a 100-round drum magazine. Infantry rarely saw these magazines and so used the standard 30-round box magazine. Brens were also issued to Allies including resistance fighters and the Nationalist Chinese Army. Some of the weapons that went to the Chinese were made in 7.92mm Mauser calibre, as the Chinese used that cartridge widely.

In action, the Bren proved its worth consistently throughout the war. In Tunisia during early 1943, Sgt James Drake of the 16th Durham Light Infantry prepared his platoon for an

enemy attack by putting a Bren on each flank of their position, "so they could fire across our front in a crossfire. I gave strict instructions that nobody must fire a shot until I said so... I waited until they had got within a hundred yards before I gave a fire order... Both the Brens started and we simply mowed them down". he later said: "The battle went on all day; by its end both Brens had bent barrels, melted by so much firing."

In Normandy, Royal Marine Commando James Kelly used his Bren against a German counter-attack. He often switched his Bren to semi-automatic so the enemy would think he was armed with a rifle. When they gathered to advance, he would switch to full-automatic and fire a burst at them.

During December 1944, Sgt Umrao Singh of the 30th Mountain Regiment, Indian Artillery, used a Bren to defend against two companies of Japanese infantry during two attacks. Wounded seven times and out of ammunition, he fought on with an iron bar until being overcome. He was found later, alive but badly wounded, ten dead Japanese soldiers around him. He earned a Victoria Cross for his bravery.

Leslie Starcevich of the 2/43rd Australian Infantry Battalion earned a Victoria Cross with his Bren in Borneo in June 1945. With his section in the lead, they encountered two Japanese machine gun nests, which opened fire. He charged both nests while firing his Bren from the hip, killing five enemy soldiers and forcing the rest to flee. The advance resumed until they ran into two more Japanese machine gun nests. Starcevich again advanced on both of them and knocked them out, killing seven more Japanese troops. This is an excellent example of how effective a skilled LMG gunner could be.

Bren Mk 1	
Calibre	.303 (7.7mm)
Magazine	30-round box
Length	45.5in (115.6cm)
Weight	22.12lb (10.03kg)
Rate of Fire	500 rpm

BELOW: A Bren group of 1st Battalion 6th East Surrey Regiment pauses near a hedgerow at Gioiella, Italy, in June 1944. Keeping the Bren supplied with ammunition was an important job for the entire section. (IWM NA16537)

Vickers Mark 1

The Vickers machine gun ranks among the most famous weapons in military history. Many will point to its solid service during World War One in the trench warfare of the Western Front. However, it went on to serve notably in World War Two to equally great effect, providing heavy machine gun support in all theatres. The Vickers actually remained in British Army service until 1968, last seeing action in Aden. While its main counterpart, the German MG42, had a rate of fire more than twice as high and was more portable, nothing could surpass the Vickers gun in the sustained fire role.

Derived from the famous Maxim gun, the British firm of Vickers purchased the Maxim company in 1896 and improved on the already good design by reducing the weight and adding a muzzle booster. This device harnessed the energy produced by the burning propellant to cycle the weapon, improving reliability. The British Army adopted the Vickers in 1912, gaining what was at the time an advanced technology weapon. After

providing sterling service in World War One, it served on until the 1930s, when some thought went into replacing it. However, World War Two was looming and the lack of a superior replacement left the Vickers in service with the British and Commonwealth armies.

The Vickers is belt-fed, using a cloth belt that feeds from the right. Photographs of Vickers in action during sustained firing often show dozens of empty belts piled up on the gun's left side. It is water-cooled, as evidenced by the large cylindrical water jacket surrounding the barrel,

Vickers Mark 1	
Calibre	.303 British
Feed	250-round belt
Length	45.5in (115.6cm)
Weight*	40lb (18.1kg) with water
Rate of Fire	500 rpm

*Tripod weighed 48.5lb (22kg)

as seen on the Browning M1917 and Soviet PM1910. This water jacket can be connected at the front by a hose to a water can, which captured water evaporated by barrel heating and helped prevent steam from rising from the weapon and giving away the firer's exact position. Even in freezing weather a machine gun's barrel will overheat during extended firing, so the water level must be maintained. The barrel could be changed in two minutes.

Like many other weapons, the Vickers went through a process of simplification during World War Two to make it easier and quicker to manufacture. The most noticeable is the water jacket. Pre-war Vickers have a water jacket made of corrugated metal, giving the jacket a ribbed appearance. Wartime guns use a smooth water jacket that sometimes had a cloth secured around it to prevent serious burns if the crew had to pick up the weapon while still hot. Insulated gloves were also issued for handling hot water jackets and barrels.

Like other machine guns, the Vickers could be used in the indirect fire role, arcing bullets through the air to land behind intervening terrain or obstacles. The Vickers excelled at this role due to its sustained fire capability. The army created and issued an indirect fire sight for this purpose, which resembles a small scope. While pinpoint accuracy could not be achieved in this mode, such firing would create what is called a 'beaten zone', where enough projectiles are falling in a given area to put anyone there at great risk. The bullets tend to land in an elliptical pattern. Such fire could be used against enemy resupply routes or to keep the enemy pinned in place. The army developed the Mk.8Z cartridge, which was streamlined for long-range firing, using a 'boat-tailed' bullet that tapered slightly at the rear. Using this ammunition, the Vickers could achieve a range of 4,500 yards in indirect mode.

British and Commonwealth forces most commonly used the Vickers in the infantry support role, mounted on a heavy tripod for stable firing. Occasionally, soldiers mounted them on vehicles such as lorries, often an improvisation to make the weapon more mobile. If a Vickers crew had sufficient ammunition, water and a spare barrel or two, they could continue firing for hours. As with other water-cooled machine guns, stories abound of Vickers crews in desperate circumstances urinating in the water jacket to keep the gun going. There are also stories of soldiers using the boiling water from a Vickers to make tea, but the water would have been mixed with oil and other substances, making this unlikely or at least unpleasant.

ABOVE: A Vickers gun in Holland, January 1945. Even in the cold conditions, the gun is hooked to its water supply to prevent overheating. It also has the indirect fire sight attached. (IWM B13619)

Vickers guns were always integrated into defence plans and even ambushes due to their firepower. Mark Rutherford served in the 2nd Infantry Division in Burma as a 19-year-old private. He recalled: "The idea was to keep going, make contact with the enemy by setting up ambush points in the jungle. We had .303 Vickers, heavy machine guns, First World War technology but deadly effective as long as you kept them cool. When you set up a camp for the night, you had to devise a secure perimeter defended by the Vickers, two-inch calibre mortars and Bren guns and then a series of watchmen whose job it was to alert the camp of any Jap [sic] intrusions."

BELOW: A Vickers team from 1st Battalion, Middlesex Regiment, fire during the fighting at Goch, Germany, February 1945. The angle of the gun indicates they are firing at long range into a beaten zone to suppress the enemy. (IWM B14757)

M1918A2 Browning Automatic Rifle

American light machine gun

ABOVE: Three US Army BAR men fire at Japanese troops in the Intramuros section of Manila in the Philippines, February 1945. Note the man kneeling behind them is loading BAR magazines. (NARA)

The Browning Automatic Rifle (BAR) served the United States military as its primary light machine gun from the end of World War One into the 1950s. Created by the famous gun designer John Browning, it was intended as a portable automatic weapon to help troops advance against heavy machine guns in the trenches. While its relatively low magazine capacity limited its value as a fire support weapon, the BAR's durability and reliability won the respect of those who carried it.

By World War II, the M1918A2 was the standard model in US service. Overall, it changed little from previous models, the primary difference being changes to its firing selection. Older BARs could fire in either semi- or fully automatic.

The M1918A2 could fire either 'slow automatic' at 350 rounds per minute (rpm) or 'fast automatic' at 550 rpm. Not all soldiers or Marines liked losing the semi-automatic feature, but a skilled user could fire single shots using the slower setting.

US Army units issued the BAR at a rate of one per squad, while the Marine Corps issued three per squad, forming three four-man fire teams with the BAR as its base of fire weapon. Army troops often acquired extra BARs to give their squads more firepower. Two or more BARs in a squad allowed the troops to maintain a constant fire at their enemy; one BAR man firing while the other loaded. Many users removed parts, such as the carrying handle and bipod, to make the weapon lighter, using the weapon more like a rifle.

Technical Sergeant Clinton Hendrick of the 17th Airborne division used his BAR during the fighting near Wesel, Germany, in March 1945. When German machine guns pinned down his platoon, Hendrick ignored their fire and advanced, firing his BAR from the hip. This inspired his fellow soldiers, who followed him and soon took the machine gun positions. When six Germans tried to flank his platoon, Hendrick spun around and killed all six with one long burst from his weapon. Next, he went with three other men to take the surrender of a German force in a nearby castle. While there, a German self-propelled gun appeared and fired at them. Though wounded, Hendrick stayed behind and used his BAR to hold off the enemy. He died of his wounds but received the Medal of Honor for his heroism.

RIGHT: A paratrooper who has just landed on the island of Corregidor in February 1945 fires at Japanese troops. Note the large ammunition belt for the BAR's magazines. (NARA)

Browning Automatic Rifle M1918A2	
Calibre	.30
Magazine	20 round box
Length	47.8in (121.4cm)
Weight	19.4lb (8.8kg)
Rate of Fire	300-450 rpm (slow setting) 500-600 rpm (fast setting)

Browning M1917

The United States fought World War One with a mix of French and British machine gun models, due to its unpreparedness. The famous weapons designer John Browning devised an effective and reliable machine gun for mass production, making two versions: the water-cooled Model 1917 and the air cooled M1919. The weapons are similar otherwise, but saw different uses. For the sustained long-range fire role, the M1917 proved ideal, similar to the British Vickers gun.

Famously, Browning demonstrated the M1917 to the US Army by training a crew of officers to operate the weapon. They proceeded to fire 20,000 rounds from the weapon without any failures (of the weapon) and only three stoppages that were due to problems with the ammunition. To further prove his design, Browning fired another 20,000 rounds with no stoppages. A second M1917 fired for 42 minutes without a stoppage. The weapon also had no small or delicate parts, and could be taken apart using a pocketsize tool, and a cartridge.

In service the M1917 saw use in battalion weapons companies as a heavy machine gun, though both US Army and US Marine organisation changed over the course of the war. Some units were issued both M1917s and M1919s, using the M1917s for defensive positions or long-range supporting fires, while the more portable M1919s were carried when advancing or attacking. The M1917 came with accessories including a tripod for stable firing, and a water can for replenishing the water jacket. The water can was not always used, depending on how long the unit expected to be in a given

location and whether heavy action was expected.

One of the most famous uses of the M1917 occurred on Guadalcanal during October 24-25, 1942. Marine Sgt John Basilone led a section of two M1917s dug in along the east bank of the Matanikau River. A Japanese regiment attacked his position. After the first day of fighting, the section was reduced to Basilone and two men. They used their M1917s against repeated Japanese attacks, which were supported by artillery, mortar, and machine gun fire. When one gun became damaged, Basilone personally retrieved a reserve weapon, and got it into action. He kept the weapons operational throughout the battle. Japanese troops who got across the shallow river past his M1917s were shot down by Basilone using his .45 pistol. Instrumental in defeating the Japanese attack, Basilone was awarded a Medal of Honor. He was killed in action on Iwo Jima on February 19, 1945.

ABOVE: A Marine fires his HMG toward Japanese positions at the base of Mount Suribachi on Iwo Jima, February 1945. (USMC)

Browning Model 1917A1	
Calibre	.30 calibre M1
Feed	250 round belt
Length	38.6in (98cm)
Weight*	32.6lb (14.8kg)
Rate of Fire	600 rpm

*103lb (47kg) loaded with tripod and water

LEFT: Two men from a US Army machine gun squad have set up their M1917 along a hedgerow in Normandy, Summer, 1944. The rear sight is folded down as the ranges in the hedgerows were often too short to need it. (NARA)

Browning Model 1919

The M1919 series machine guns were the air-cooled version of the M1917 (see page 65). Too late for World War One, the M1919 went on become the primary medium machine gun of all US forces during World War Two and through the late 1950s. A few models continued in service into the 1970s. The BAR (see page 64) filled the light machine gun (LMG) role, while the water cooled M1917 filled the heavy machine gun role. Many wartime US documents refer to the M1919 simply as the medium machine gun, or MMG, although it is also referred to as an LMG.

During the 1920s and 30s, the M1919 went through an evolution until the M1919A4 appeared in 1935. The weapon saw limited issue due to slow production until the war started, when manufacture rapidly increased. Several companies produced over 430,000 M1919s during the war. Most saw use with the infantry in machine gun or weapons platoons at the company level, many of which went through reorganisations during the war. Airborne companies were an exception as they did not have weapons platoons – each rifle platoon had two rifle

squads; each squad had one M1919 crewed by a gunner, assistant and ammunition bearer.

Though sometimes called an LMG, the M1919A4 did not really meet the definition as it was too heavy, and was tripod mounted. With no other design available, the army modified an M1919A4 with a lighter barrel, a removable shoulder stock, a bipod, and a carrying handle. The finished

Browning Model 1919A4	
Calibre	.30 calibre M1
Feed	250 round belt
Length	41in (104.1cm)
Weight*	31lb (14.1kg)
Rate of Fire	600 rpm

*32.5lb (14.7kg) for M1919A6

version weighed only slightly more than the M1919A4 without the tripod, and was designated the M1919A6. Though not a perfect solution, it was the best available and entered widespread service in late 1944. It could be mounted on a tripod if needed. M1919s also saw wide use on tanks and vehicles.

Richard Lacey, a soldier in the US 30th Infantry Division, wrote of the effectiveness of his machine gun, describing a battle in Holland. He was part of a two-gun section set up to cover a road. The next morning, a company of over 100 Germans came down the road, unaware of the Americans. "When they got close enough, about 75 yards from us, we opened up with our machine guns. We had a perfect field of fire and they didn't have anywhere to go. The fighting only lasted about ten minutes and they surrendered. We killed 18, wounded 13 and captured about 75 of them."

M2 .50 Cal. Machine Gun

The Ma Deuce

The US Browning M2 .50 calibre heavy machine gun officially entered service in 1933, though its initial development began at the end of World War One. Too late for that conflict, its designer, the famous John Browning, refined it into a weapon that is still in use today around the world, with every attempt to replace it failing.

The M2, nicknamed the 'Ma Deuce' by US troops, but often just called the 'fifty-cal,' proved versatile in service. The US Army initially acquired it as an anti-aircraft and anti-tank weapon, though its anti-tank value was minimal even early in the war. From there it was mounted on armoured vehicles, aircraft, ships, patrol boats, and specialised anti-aircraft mountings, with up to four machine guns, known as a 'quad-fifty.'

In practice, the M2 seldom saw direct use by US infantry due to its size and weight, the exception being armoured infantry, who often had

M2 .50 calibre Machine Gun	
Calibre	.50 Browning Machine Gun (12.7mm)
Feed	100 round belts
Length	65.1in (165.4cm)
Weight*	84lb (38.1kg)
Rate of Fire	450-600 rpm

*128lb (58kg) with tripod and traverse and elevation mechanism

ABOVE: A soldier mans a halftrack-mounted M2 at Remagen, Germany, March 1945. After crossing the Rhine, US troops at Remagen held a perimeter against German counterattacks for days. (NARA)

the M2 mounted on their halftracks. This gave them a distinct firepower advantage over German infantry, who had nothing comparable. Other US infantry units only had the M2 at the battalion or regimental level as an anti-aircraft defence weapon. However, anti-aircraft, and other supporting units which had large numbers of M2s, used them frequently to support infantry in action with often brutal results.

One American commander, who used his M2s against opposing German machine guns, reported "opposing German machine guns had ceased their fire due to stoppages...of manpower." Two halftracks mounting quad-fifties would clear a street by racing down it, firing into each building, turning around at the end of the street and going back, doing the same thing. Afterwards infantry would mop up the survivors. In another instance, 30 Germans attacked a quad-fifty in Mons, Belgium; one minute later, 25 were dead.

Famous US soldier Lt Audie Murphy earned a Medal of Honor with an M2 on January 26, 1945. Under attack by a German force of tanks and infantry, he directed his men to cover while he called in artillery strikes. Next, he climbed atop a burning American tank destroyer and used its M2 to hold off waves of infantry for an hour, ignoring a leg wound, and inflicting 50 casualties on the Germans. He refused medical help, and led a counterattack that forced the Germans to retreat.

LEFT: A halftrack crew prepares their M2 as they wait their turn to board a ship for Normandy, 1944. Having a .50 for fire support proved a huge advantage to US armoured infantry. (NARA)

Soviet weapons designer Vasily Degtyaryov created a range of automatic weapons for the Red Army. The DP series machine guns were among the most successful of these, serving as the infantry's standard light machine gun (LMG). The Soviets referred to the weapon as the DP-27; however, in the west it is sometimes called the DP-28.

Degtyaryov designed the weapon in the 1920s and it was improved during production in the 1930s. This included the addition of a quick-change barrel to solve the problem of overheating common to LMGs. It was heavy, but solid and reliable, firing from a rotating pan magazine fitted atop the receiver, similar to the World War One-era Lewis Gun. Soviet troops nicknamed it the 'record player' due to this pan. Its relatively low rate of fire made it easier to control, and the DP-27 was also accurate.

DP-27

Soviet light machine gun

At the beginning of the war, Soviet rifle squads had one DP-27 each; later in the war infantry squads were organised into Type A and B squads, with the B Squad having two DP-27s. The gunner carried the weapon with one magazine, while the assistant gunner carried three magazines. More magazines could be spread among the squad's riflemen, although they were heavy, and carrying too many would overburden them.

In practice, DP-27 crews moved often in combat as their weapon drew fire once identified. In the attack, they suppressed the enemy while the riflemen moved up. In the defence, the DP-27 served as the base of the squad's firepower. German troops noted that in the defence, Soviet troops often waited until their opponents came within 100m before using their LMGs, to maximize their effect, and pin the Germans down. The Soviet troops learned that opening fire from too great a distance meant German troops would usually withdraw and call in artillery.

Machine gunner Nikolai Dyakonov used his DP-27 expertly in difficult circumstances in July 1944. In the leading wave of an assault crossing of the Bug River, Dyakonov and some other Soviet troops, seized high ground on the West Bank. For two days the Germans attacked the group, trying desperately to destroy the bridgehead. Each time, Dyakonov used his DP-27 to throw the enemy back. When other Soviet troops finally relieved the small group, over 200 German dead surrounded their position, most of them felled by the LMG's deadly fire. Dyakonov became a Hero of the Soviet Union, and his DP-27 is now on display in Moscow's Central Museum of the Armed Forces in present-day Russia.

RIGHT: A DP-27 gunner takes cover in a trench, September 1941. Even in such muddy conditions, his weapon will work with just a modicum of maintenance. (RUSSIAN ARCHIVES)

BELOW: Infantry of the 3rd Ukrainian Front advance in an Eastern European town, covered by a DP-27 machine gun team in January 1945. (RUSSIAN ARCHIVES)

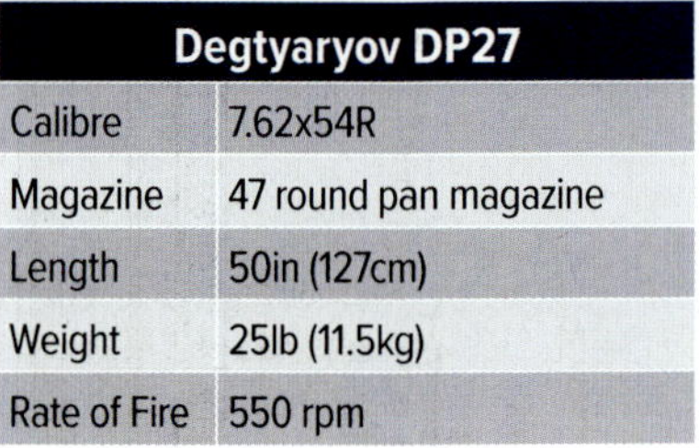

Degtyaryov DP27	
Calibre	7.62x54R
Magazine	47 round pan magazine
Length	50in (127cm)
Weight	25lb (11.5kg)
Rate of Fire	550 rpm

Maxim M1910/30

The Soviet's venerable but effective machine gun

PM1910/30	
Calibre	7.62x54R
Feed	250 round cloth belt
Length	43.6in (220.7cm)
Weight	99.65lb (45.2kg) with gun shield and mount
Rate of Fire	520-600 rpm

LEFT: An M1910/30 crew operates their weapon from a foxhole on the Eastern Front. The man in the foreground carries a spare ammunition can along with his PPSh41 submachine gun. (RUSSIAN ARCHIVES)

The belt-fed M1910 series served as the Red Army's standard medium machine gun during World War Two. A derivative of the famous Maxim Gun, this heavy, water-cooled weapon was known for its durability, and the steady rate at which it could lay down heavy and consistent fire.

The modernized M1910/30 incorporated several improvements to the mechanism to increase performance and ease of manufacture. Soviet industry produced more M1910/30s than any other machine gun, with 270,000 made during 1944 alone. For portability it was mounted on a small, wheeled carriage which could easily be pushed or pulled by its crew; some of these carriages had legs which could be extended into a tripod or anti-aircraft mount.

In action, the M1910/30 had a crew of five: commander, gunner, assistant gunner, observer and ammunition bearer. Sometimes the squad had a horse to tow the weapon and would then have a horse driver. A Soviet machine gun squad's two primary roles were to support the infantry during an attack and to defend positions. The M1910/30 excelled at both, capable of stable long-range fire support for long periods. Finland used many Soviet-pattern weapons and also employed Maxim-type weapons throughout the war.

As a water-cooled weapon, it could fire long bursts, but in practice this was forbidden. Long bursts gave away the gun's position and enabled return fire which might kill or suppress the crew. The gun's ability to lay down heavy fire meant German troops called in artillery or other heavy fire when they located one. Most M1910/30s had a gun shield attached to its mounting to help protect the gunner.

While Soviet troops prized the M1910/30 for its reliability and firepower, it had its drawbacks. Its heavy overall weight made it hard to keep up with rapidly advancing infantry. Like other water-cooled weapons, the water supply added even more weight and if the water jacket was hit, the resulting leak led to rapid overheating. Many weapons had a large port in the water jacket so ice or snow could be packed into it if needed. As the war progressed and the Red Army became more capable of fast, mobile operations, air-cooled weapons became more prevalent.

The M1910/30 has proven long-lived beyond the war. Tens of thousands are in use in the present Ukraine War, dug into static defensive positions or mounted on vehicles to solve the portability issue.

LEFT: The Finns also used Maxim guns, often captured Soviet weapons. This Finnish gun has a port atop the water jacket for inserting snow, and the weapon is mounted on a sled for easy transport in the snow. (SA-KUVA)

MG34

The first general-purpose machine gun

Though the term did not see use during the war, the MG34 is the first of what would become known as the General-Purpose Machine Gun (GPMG). The German term 'einheitsmaschinengewehr' translates to 'universal machine gun'. Their idea envisioned a single machine gun design for infantry use, heavy fire support, vehicle mounting, and the anti-aircraft role.

Designers set out to create a simple weapon which was easy to maintain in the field and used several innovative features, many of which are now standard. Importantly, the MG34 incorporated a quick-change barrel which allowed a hot barrel to be quickly replaced by a spare barrel to prevent overheating. The hot barrel was set aside to cool and then could be rotated with the spare to keep the gun action longer during prolonged firing. The crew changed barrels by flipping a latch and rotating the receiver down and to the right. The barrel could be removed from the rear of the barrel shroud. After pushing in a new barrel, the receiver was rotated back into place, and firing could resume.

One requirement specified the ability to fire semi-automatically.

To achieve this without a selector lever mechanism, the design used a double crescent trigger. The firer used the upper portion of the trigger to fire single shots and the lower portion for automatic fire. For portability, the MG34 used a bipod attached near the muzzle – common now but still a new concept for machine guns, even in the 1930s. For sustained fire, a tripod called the Lafette 34 was available, and it could be adjusted in height to act as an anti-aircraft mount. A sight for indirect fire could be fitted to the receiver.

The MG34 used a reusable metal ammunition belt with metal links connected by wire loops so it did not disintegrate after firing, as with most modern designs. Each belt held 50 rounds and five came in one ammunition box; the belts could be

RIGHT: A German MG34 machine gun team on the Eastern Front in June 1943, set up next to a knocked out Soviet T-34 tank. The open terrain provides a large field of fire. (BUNDESARCHIV BILD 101I-219-0562A-22)

BELOW: Soldiers of the Grossdeutschland Regiment fire at retreating Russians in November 1941. Firing while using the assistant's shoulder for stability was used for shooting at sudden or fleeting targets. (BUNDESARCHIV BILD 183-B14493)

MG-34	
Calibre	7.92mm
Feed	50 or 75 round drum, 50 to 250 round belt
Length	48in (121.9cm)
Weight	25.4lb (11.5kg) with bipod
Rate of Fire	800-900 rpm

linked together to make a 250-round belt. The weapon could also use 50 or 75 round drums, providing a ready ammunition supply for the gunner. These were useful when advancing or patrolling, so the gun could be brought into action quickly without the assistants having to load the weapon from a carried box.

Once in service, the MG34 proved well-made, reliable and effective. Most armies of the period kept belt-fed machine guns in company or battalion-level weapons platoons. The Germans issued MG34s to rifle squads, with a three-soldier machine gun team providing the firepower for the squad, enabling the six-man rifle team and the squad leader to manoeuvre as needed. Even armies with machine guns at squad level issued weapons like the Bren or BAR, which were excellent designs in their own right, but incapable of sustained fire. This gave German infantry a decided firepower advantage at the squad and platoon level.

The MG34's main disadvantage arose from its high quality. It required extensive machining, which made it too expensive and time consuming for the mass production needed to feed the needs of the massive German military machine. The need to make versions of the MG34 for aircraft and tanks made the problem worse for the infantry. This is partly why the MG42 (see page 74) replaced the MG34 for infantry use, though the MG34 stayed in production for the rest of the war as a vehicle

weapon. Despite the MG42's qualities, demand stayed high for the MG34.

Gunter Koschorrek served as a machine gunner on the Eastern Front. He wrote a memoir describing his experiences. During his unit's escape from the Stalingrad encirclement in late 1942, his company came under attack by a Soviet force. Taking over an MG34 from a wounded comrade, he acted as a gunner for the first time against the charging Soviets. "This is my chance! I immediately get behind the machine gun and fire some short, carefully aimed bursts, just as I learned how. I aim into the mass of the charging Soviet infantry... My aim is good, and several of the brown clad figures fall to the ground."

As the attack continued, Koschorrek had to change his overheated barrel after a jam, burning his hand on the hot metal. He ignored the pain and continued firing. "Our machine gun bursts rip openings in their ranks. Dead and wounded are hitting the ground all the time. But more of them are coming through the haze..." When two MG34s to his right stop firing, the Soviets move toward that flank. "... I continue to fire into it as [the Soviet unit] moves toward the right." The battle turned in favour of the Germans when a 20mm quad anti-aircraft gun fired on the Soviets. Joined by the MG34s, this proved too much for the Soviet unit, which retreated.

ABOVE: This drawing of an infantryman with a slung MG34 was made by a German combat artist and later captured by American troops. (NARA)

LEFT: Waffen-SS troops from the 'Wiking' Division fire an MG34 from the anti-aircraft mount in a Soviet Village. Lowering the bipod legs helped heat radiate away from the barrel. (POLISH NATIONAL ARCHIVES)

MG42

metal stampings replaced complex and expensive machining wherever possible. The designers created the MG42's operating mechanism by combining the best features from other weapons and their own ideas gained from field use of the MG34. It also featured a quick-change barrel and could be mounted on a tripod for sustained fire, though in field use the bipod was much handier for troops on the move.

The resulting weapon proved sturdy, reliable and effective. Its high rate of fire made shooting a burst sound like tearing a bedsheet, with the rounds firing so close together it was difficult to separate the sound of each round firing. Allied troops often mentioned how frightening the mere sound of an MG 42 firing at them could be, both the sound of the machine gun and sound of a full burst of 7.92mm bullets cracking past in the air around them. This was only made worse if any of those bullets struck home.

Most Allied machine guns had firing rates of only half that of the MG42. This made it easy to distinguish who was firing but

ABOVE: An MG42 set up on the Eastern Front, January 1944. The assistant, armed with a StG44 rifle, is using binoculars to search for targets while using the tree for concealment. (BUNDESARCHIV BILD 101I-691-0244-11)

The Germans invented the concept of a GPMG with the MG34 (see page 72) and refined it with the MG42. As good as the MG34 was, the MG42 became the standard German machine gun of the war, feared and respected by Allied troops. The MG42 is undoubtedly one of the best weapons designs to emerge from the war, and continues in service with many armies today with minimal modifications or updates. Its nickname, 'Hitler's buzzsaw', is a grim testament to the carnage it could wreak in mere seconds.

Even in 1937, the German military recognised the MG34 was simply too expensive to manufacture in large numbers during wartime and sought a simplified weapon to serve as a squad machine gun. As with many other wartime designs,

RIGHT: This defensive position overlooks the Leopold Canal in the Scheldt River region in October 1944. This MG42 can cover distant high ground across the flooded areas. (POLISH NATIONAL ARCHIVE)

risky to use a captured gun unless every friendly soldier in the area knew you had one. Even so, it saw frequent use when captured by

frontline troops who had enough ammunition for it. One often-overlooked problem with the MG42 came with its rate of fire. A machine gun which fires twice as fast uses up its ammunition supply twice as fast so keeping an MG42 in action required steady resupply.

The MG42 first saw action in North Africa and the Soviet Union in late 1942. The weapon quickly developed a good reputation among its users and a fearsome one among Allied troops. The US Army even experimented with copying the MG42, rechambered for US .30 calibre ammunition. The German Army issued the weapon exclusively to frontline troops until late in the war, when its organisation began to break down. It never entirely replaced the MG34, which remained in use in armoured vehicles, but infantry generally preferred the MG42.

After his unit traded in its MG34s for the MG42 in 1943, Gunter Koschorrek used them in action on the Eastern Front. His unit set up their two MG42s at the edge of a Russian village overlooking a small hollow and some depressions where Soviet troops hid from view. When they attacked, the German machine guns tore into them. "We get our

first sight of the attackers when their earth-coloured helmets appear out of the shallow depression. The first waves are mown down by the murderous fire from our two [MG42s], and those behind now fall back into the hollow."

After repelling this assault, Koschorrek was horrified to hear the Soviet commissar blowing a whistle and ordering the remaining Soviet troops to attack again. When they obeyed, Koschorrek felt sympathy for their situation, but had to fire into them again. "Because of the firepower of our two MG42s, at a range of about 50 metres, the attackers have little chance of getting out of the hollow and certainly none at all of storming up the hillock to our positions… We fire as soon as we can see their torsos; anyone who manages to come up over the edge of the hollow can't get further than one or two paces before he is hit." The battle ended when two German flamethrower tanks arrived and Koschorrek watched in horror as the remaining Soviet troops burned to death.

British airborne officer Capt Eric Mackay had a close call with an MG42 at Arnhem during the night of September 17-18, 1944. His unit became involved in heavy fighting in the buildings on the east side of the ramp to Arnhem Bridge. A German soldier "…brought a [MG42] and poked it right through the window spraying the room. I was standing there with my .45 and just pushed it in his mouth and pulled the trigger…" Mackay then took the MG42 and turned it on the German soldiers outside.

MG42	
Calibre	7.92mm
Feed	50 to 250 round belt
Length	48in (122cm)
Weight	25.4 lb (11.5kg) with bipod
Rate of Fire	1,200rpm

LEFT: An MG42 gunner loads his weapon in a defensive position overlooking the Saar River in 1944. (POLISH NATIONAL ARCHIVE)

BELOW: Three Volkssturm militia troops man an MG42 along the Oder River in February 1945. The soldier in the foreground has a Gustloff Volkssturmgewehr, a crude rifle made in the last months of the war. (BUNDESARCHIV BILD 183-J28732)

Hand Grenades

Explosive firepower for the infantry

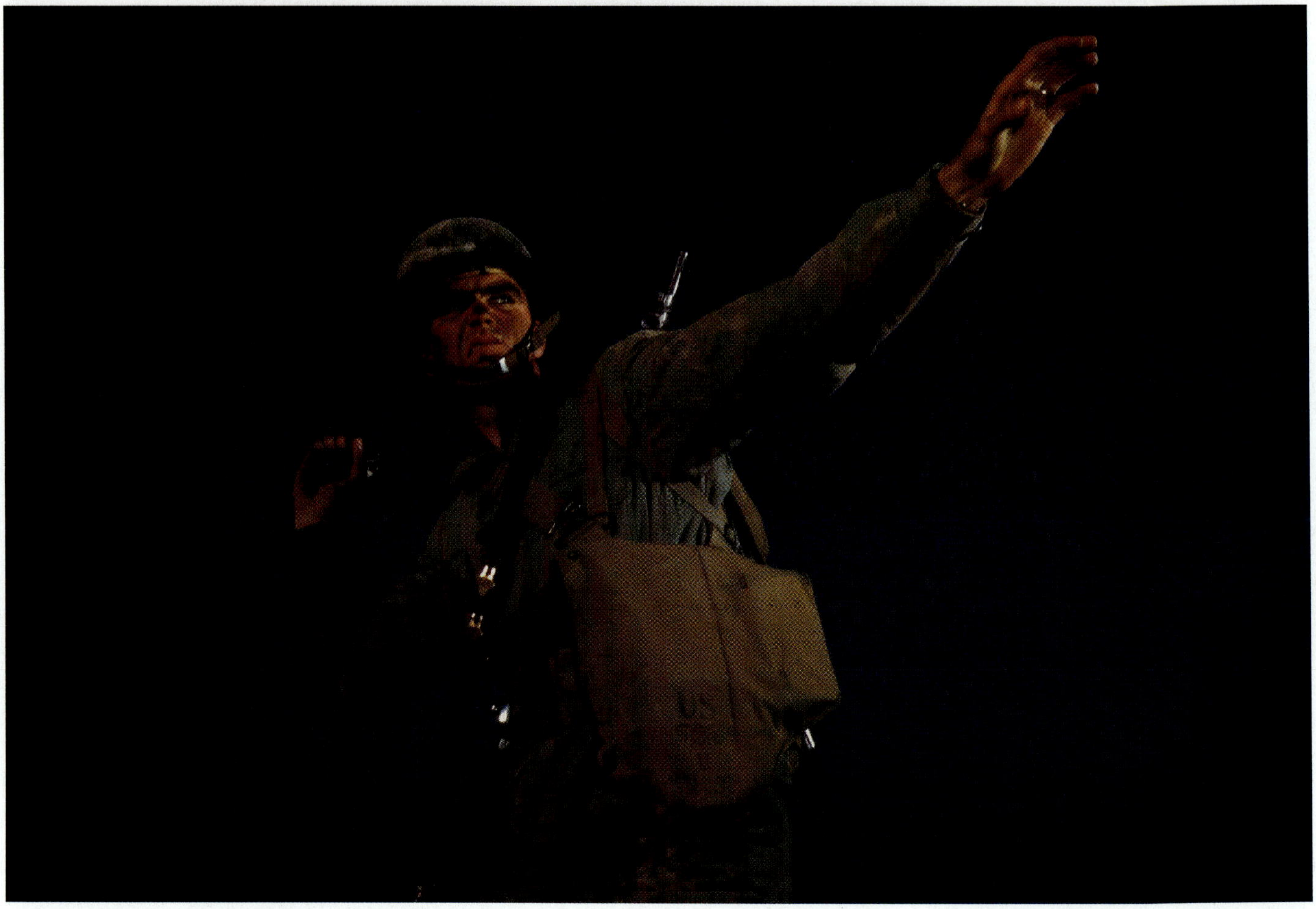

ABOVE: This posed photograph shows an American soldier in training, preparing to throw a grenade. He has his M1903 rifle slung across his back, so it won't interfere with his throw. (NARA)

Hand grenades have existed for centuries, serving as a small handheld explosive weapon for infantry use. While soldiers always preferred to let mortars, artillery, tanks or aircraft pave the way, such assets were not always available; sometimes the infantryman had to do the job themselves with a grenade. During the war there were dozens of different types of grenades in service with the combatant nations, so it is not possible to describe all of them here. Instead, we give the reader an overview of the weapon with a few interesting examples.

In general, hand grenades have a metal body small enough to be held in one hand. Some grenades had a wooden handle attached to the grenade body to aid in throwing. Each has a filler of explosives, chemicals, or a flammable substance, depending on the type of grenade. To ignite the grenade, it must have a fuze that must be armed and once activated, give the thrower a set amount of time to throw it. The fuze is the most complex part of the grenade, as it must be reliable enough to not detonate the grenade too early or too late.

Four to six seconds was normal for most grenades at the time, but manufacturing tolerances of the time could easily add or subtract a half second. Soldiers were naturally nervous handling grenades, hoping the factory workers had done their job properly. Some soldiers would try to 'cook off' a grenade, waiting a second or two to throw it so the target would not have time to escape its blast or throw it back.

Most fuzes were activated by pulling a pin, starting the detonation

RIGHT: A German soldier prepares to throw a grenade on the Eastern Front, 1941. He will not be able to throw it very far from the prone position. (NARA)

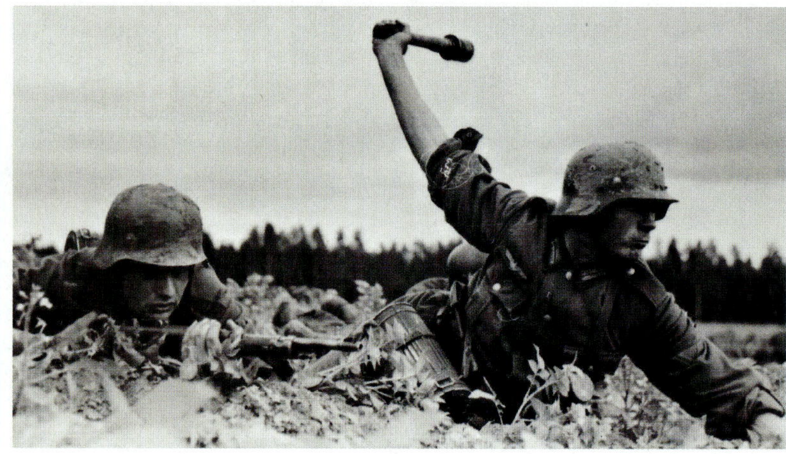

sequence as the grenade was thrown, when its safety lever disengaged. Some grenades, such as the German Stielhandgranate 24, used a weighted string which was pulled before throwing. Some Japanese hand grenades had percussion fuzes. After pulling the pin, the grenade had to be struck against a solid object, such as the soldier's helmet, and then thrown.

During World War Two several different types of hand grenade were in general use.

Fragmentation. This type possesses a relatively thick metal body, usually simple cast iron, which is shredded into fragments by the grenade's explosive charge. These fragments are the primary cause of casualties, although they can also cause wounds or damage by blast and heat effects of the bursting charge.

Examples include the British No 36 Mills grenade and the American Mk II, commonly called the 'pineapple'. This was due to its shape and because early in the war, US grenades were painted yellow. This made them highly visible, and soon they were repainted in olive drab. While the Germans were known for their wooden handled stick grenades, nicknamed 'potato mashers', they also used the smaller M39 'egg grenade', which was made in larger numbers.

Explosive. Sometimes called a concussion grenade, these relied on a larger explosive charge to cause casualties or do damage with little to no fragmentation. Intended for offensive actions and attacks, these weapons were considered less deadly and so could be used by advancing troops with less risk of injury from their own weapon. The grenades produced a considerable concussion effect in closed spaces, so they were often used for attacking bunkers and similar defences.

Smoke. Smoke grenades were used to obscure troops from enemy observation, sometimes to cover a movement or to lessen the accuracy of enemy fire. Coloured smoke grenades were used for signalling.

Anti-tank. Designed to pierce armour, anti-tank grenades proved of limited effectiveness, particularly as tank armour improved during the war. However, they provided a last-ditch weapon for infantry under tank attack. Several designs, such as the Soviet RPG43, used the then-new shaped charge warhead design to increase their penetrating power. However, they had to strike at the proper angle to function effectively. When it did so, an RPG43 could penetrate 3in (76mm) of armour.

The British developed the No 75 Hawkins grenade, which could disable a tank if thrown under its treads. Several could be tied together and dragged across a road as the tank approached. The No 82 Gammon grenade, often called the Gammon bomb, could be configured for anti-personnel or anti-tank use, depending on how much explosive was added.

Incendiary. These grenades were rarely used in combat, as they were more useful for destroying equipment and starting fires, since they lack an explosive charge. Improvised incendiary weapons, such as Molotov cocktails, were much more common on the battlefield.

ABOVE: Two 'Tommys' of the 1st Queen's Own Royal West Kent Regiment man a trench in France, April 1940. They have several No 36 Mills Bombs at the ready for close combat. (IWM F3552)

TOP: Japanese troops hid this Type 97 grenade inside a cabbage on Okinawa as a trap for American troops. (NARA)

LEFT: Marines throw grenades at dug-in Japanese troops on Saipan, January 1944. One grenade is in the air at top centre, while the second emits smoke in the hand of the second thrower. (NARA)

Rifle Grenades

Ranged firepower

Rifle grenades are often overlooked in studies of the weapons of World War Two, but they were widely used by infantry at the time. They were similar in power to standard hand grenades, but being fired from a launcher adapted to an infantry rifle extended their range beyond throwing distance. Some combatants, such as the Japanese, used grenade designs which could function as either a hand or rifle grenade using a special adaptor.

As the war continued, most rifle grenades came to resemble small rockets, similar to an anti-tank rocket. However, they did not have an internal motor, being propelled by the force of the rifle firing. Some designs required a blank cartridge; the gases produced by firing propelled the grenade. A few designs could function with live ammunition or using special cartridges with wooden bullets. Rifle grenade firing ranges varied from 60 to 200yds (50-180m).

Both anti-personnel and anti-tank rifle grenades existed. Anti-personnel types used blast and fragmentation effects just as with a hand grenade. The anti-tank models had limited armour penetration due to their size but could damage a tank by hitting the side, rear or top armour. Most had shaped-charge warheads. They proved more effective against lighter vehicles, such as armoured cars and halftracks.

Semi-automatic weapons like the M1 Garand required specialised grenade launcher adaptors to function properly. In the first two years of the war, US infantry squads had to have one soldier equipped with the older bolt action M1903 Springfield to launch rifle grenades. By 1944, grenade launcher attachments for the M1 Garand

and M1 Carbine became available. With an assistant to load grenades, a soldier could achieve a high rate of fire with rifle grenades, up to 20 rounds a minute.

The German Army fielded a unique rifle grenade designed to deliver propaganda leaflets. A thin metal body with a removeable nose cap contained the leaflets. Upon firing with a blank cartridge, a time fuze caused the grenade to open after nine seconds, scattering the leaflets.

Rifle grenades filled a gap between the hand grenade and light mortar (see page 88). They gave infantry added firepower, although they were bulkier than a hand grenade and added weight to the soldier's load. Keeping an enemy out of hand grenade range could be an advantage in itself.

ABOVE: A member of the British Home Guard demonstrates one method for bracing the rifle when firing a grenade, August 1942. (IWM H22061)

LEFT: A German soldier on the Eastern Front stands ready to fire a rifle grenade while his colleague searches for targets. (POLISH NATIONAL ARCHIVES)

BELOW: An American lieutenant from the 37th Infantry Division, serving in the Pacific, demonstrates the proper way to hold a rifle for firing the rifle grenade. Note the adaptor on the end of the barrel. (NARA)

Mines

Landmines ranked among the most effective anti-personnel weapons of World War Two. They were simultaneously among the most hated and feared. The combatant nations laid tens of millions of mines during the war. Infantrymen loathed mines because they were a hidden threat and were dangerous, and time-consuming to remove. Even 80 years later, untold thousands of mines from 1939-1945 are still in the ground around the world, posing a hidden threat to people unaware they are even there.

There were many models and types of landmines, mostly divided simply into anti-personnel and anti-tank categories. They could be set off by pressure, tripwires, or detonated by remote control. Most often they were laid by engineers, though infantry were trained to emplace and clear them, frequently assisting the trained engineers as minefields could include thousands of individual mines. Modern films often show soldiers stepping on mines with an audible clicking noise, then being stuck in place for fear of the mine detonating when he steps off it, while his mates try to devise a way to save him. This is a dramatic device because mines explode upon being triggered, not when the pressure on them is released.

Anti-personnel mines included standard types which simply exploded when stepped on, or bounding mines such as the German S-mine. Nicknamed the 'Bouncing Betty', the S-mine had several prongs atop the fuse, which triggered three or four seconds after activation. The mine then sprung into the air to a height of about 3ft (1m) before exploding, spraying shrapnel in a wide area. Anti-personnel mines could be smaller as less explosive was needed to cause casualties; the aim of these mines was often to wound, as wounded soldiers require several able soldiers to tend and evacuate them, weakening a unit for a time.

Anti-tank mines had to be larger to hold enough high explosive to damage armoured vehicles. They often only disabled them by destroying tracks and road wheels, but it was effective enough as it took the vehicle out of action until repaired.

Mines were often laid with devious ingenuity. They could be booby trapped to make disarming them more difficult, or wired together in a series so tampering with one might set off several. Many mines had detonators which fit into the top of the mine, and the minelayers would bury them upside down so mine clearing troops could not reach them. The Soviets frequently dug up mines in front of German positions and relaid them elsewhere. A common German trick involved burying tin cans. Their opponents would waste time clearing them and might miss the actual mines, which would be scattered among the cans.

Minefields delayed advancing troops, forcing them to slowly clear the mines or wait for engineers. During a retreat, mines were laid to slow any pursuers. Mines in front of a defensive position also slowed the enemy. These tactics had greater effect when the minefield was under observation and covered by machine guns, mortars, and artillery. When troops or armoured vehicles hit a minefield, they tend to stop. This makes them prime targets for other weapons. Troops will naturally withdraw from a minefield, so other minefields can be laid in whatever direction it seems likely those troops will move, pushing those troops into a killing zone.

Mine detectors, originally a Polish invention later given to the British,

quickly entered service in large numbers. Some armies countered by producing mines with little or no metal content. Infantry could probe for mines by using a bayonet or stick to feel for mines. Once found, they could be marked for avoidance and later recovery. Troops on punishment duty, such as in a penal battalion, were used in the mine clearing role in the German and Soviet armies.

As with their other weapons, soldiers could become very creative in deploying mines. One German report stated: "When we took Kiev and Vyborg in 1941... the Russians used remote (radio) controlled mines for blowing up entire blocks

of houses as soon as the enemy entered them. The ignition apparatus included a clock, which could be heard with sensitive sound detectors and led to the discovery of the ignition apparatus." The Soviets were also well-known for booby trapping anything they thought a German soldier might touch or pick up.

Most armies made extensive efforts to train their soldiers on the dangers of mines. The British Army published a series of booklets on lessons learned in action (other armies did this as well), including mines. One 1942 edition about North Africa stated: "The mines were laid at very irregular intervals, but always on or near a desert trail... in some instances, places where mines were laid showed signs of the earth having been disturbed, but in others there was no such indication... Dummy minefields were also encountered... and contained tins sunk into the ground with occasional booby traps attached to them. Gaps between dummy minefields were invariably sown with live mines."

ABOVE: Three Soviet soldiers cross a stream to lay captured German mines on the opposite shore. The nearest two soldiers are carrying captured Mauser rifles. (RUSSIAN ARCHIVES PUBLIC DOMAIN)

LEFT: A Soviet mine clearing team uncover a mine in the Donbas, July 1943. Mines were often laid near water crossings to delay the enemy. (RIAN ARCHIVE 67318)

LEFT: A Finnish soldier on a ski patrol lays a mine for any following Soviet troops, 1944. (SA KUVA)

The Bayonet

Enduring symbol of the infantry

ABOVE: Sunlight penetrating the jungle canopy has darkened the outline of these American soldiers on Bougainville, March 1944. Bayonets could be useful in close terrain as enemy soldiers could appear at short distances. (NARA)

Every infantry recruit has learned about the bayonet. They learned how to thrust and parry with a bayonet on the end of their rifle, engendered with the 'spirit of the bayonet' as part of the infantryman's duty to close with and defeat their enemy at close quarters. Referred to as 'cold steel', the bayonet provided a link back to the days of musketry and pike, and every infantryman was issued one as part of their kit.

The problem was, by World War Two, the bayonet as a weapon was obsolete. When soldiers in World War One fixed bayonets and went over the top, artillery and machine guns had already relegated it to history, although armies of the period had not yet accepted that fact. Soldiers occasionally employed them against an enemy, but as a battlefield weapon their impact was negligible. When used, it was often during night actions or in close quarters combat, where soldiers got close enough to use them.

Prior to the war, most bayonets were long bladed, either in a sword or spike pattern. These were unwieldy, especially in close quarters; heavy and hard to carry. By World War Two, bayonets were still issued, but in a smaller knife-pattern, making them useful as tools as well as weapons. Even the spike bayonets were shortened to manageable lengths. This actually made the bayonet more useful for hand-to-hand combat, as a shorter blade made it easier to use.

The Japanese Army continued to use bayonets as a primary weapon for much of the war, as their doctrine specified close combat as a battle-winning tactic, with other arms existing to enable that close fight. While this tactic had some success against badly equipped forces in China, for example, it fared poorly against modern armies. Banzai charges against Allied troops typically ended with the attacking forces destroyed for little result.

Despite their limited utility as a weapon, most soldiers had a bayonet, so they were sought after souvenirs. While not as desirable as a pistol or Japanese sword, a bayonet was a weapon and thus desirable.

RIGHT: Commonwealth troops advance past a dead Italian soldier in June 1942. Their bayonets are the older long-bladed pattern first issued during the Great War, two decades earlier. (IWM E12922)

Flamethrowers

Short-ranged incendiary weapon

Handheld flamethrowers saw widespread use throughout the war. Often the soldiers employing them were combat engineers or other specialists rather than infantrymen. These flamethrowers had limited range and fuel capacity, so many armies installed larger models in tanks and other armoured vehicles.

Soldier-carried flamethrowers have a storage tank system mounted on the soldier's back. These tanks carry the flammable liquid and an inert propellant gas such as nitrogen. The tanks connect via flexible tube to the gun system, which contains an igniter to light the flammable liquid when it is propelled towards the target during firing. These weapons typically had ranges from 25 to 40yds.

Notably, flamethrowers do not explode when hit by gunfire as shown in films. Shooting holes in the tanks simply makes the contents leak out. Standard bullets will not ignite the fuel, although specialised incendiary ammunition could do so.

Flamethrowers were typically used against fixed fortifications such as bunkers and defended caves. Due to the weapon's range limitations, the operator had to close the range, often under fire. Carrying the heavy apparatus was also very fatiguing. Flamethrower operators stood out on the battlefield and frequently drew fire from anyone within range, due to the natural fear of burning to death.

LEFT: A German soldier uses a Flammenwerfer 41 flamethrower on the Eastern Front in 1941 or 1942. He is setting fire to a building. (AWM 044602)

There are undocumented stories of flamethrower operators being summarily killed if captured, though these claims have also been made about machine gunners, snipers, and other specialists. It is known that snipers considered flamethrowers a primary target. The Red Army issued a flamethrower in which the gun system was disguised as a rifle and the tanks as a standard issue backpack to prevent snipers from recognizing it.

Once within range, wind had to be considered to prevent the flames being blown back towards the firer. A stream of flame could be fired, or a stream of unignited fuel. If being doused in fuel failed to convince the defenders to surrender, a burst of flame decided the issue. American troops found that Germans would usually surrender but Japanese would not. In bunkers and caves the flames could also suffocate the occupants by consuming the available oxygen. Since flamethrowers had limited fuel, they were rarely used to kill soldiers in the open as shown in films. Such troops could easily be shot, saving the flamethrower for use against fortifications.

BELOW: A US Marine uses a flamethrower on a Japanese fortification on Iwo Jima. The other Marines are standing by to engage anyone who runs out to escape the flames. (USMC)

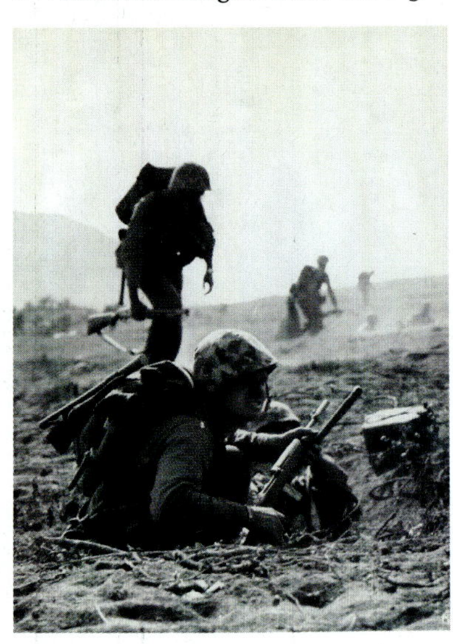

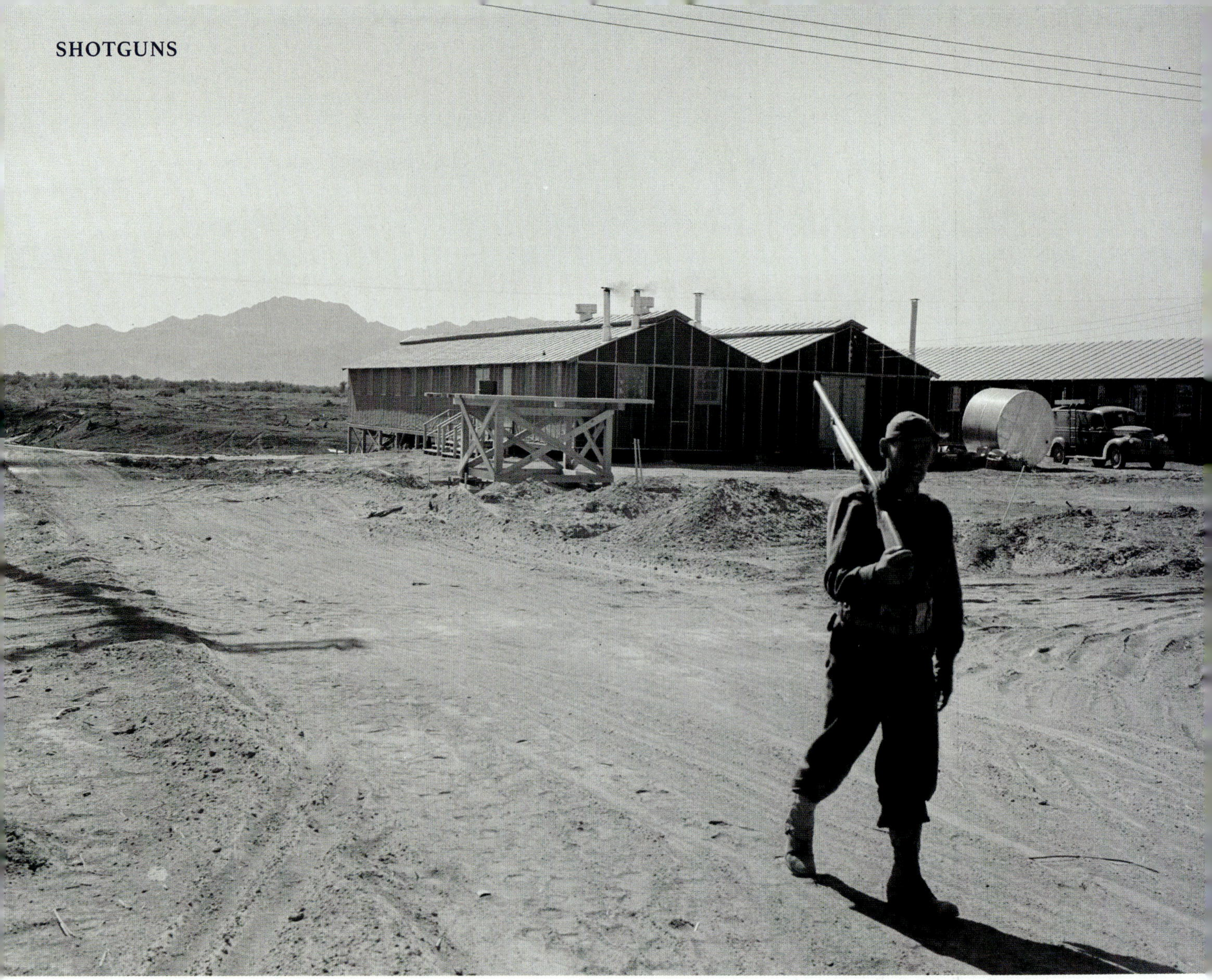

Shotguns

Simple firepower

ABOVE: As rifles were in short supply in 1942, many sentries in the United States walked their posts with shotguns. This soldier's main job was to prevent local civilians from stealing food from the 'chow hall' in the background. (NARA)

RIGHT: US Marines move inland at Iwo Jima, February 1945. The Marine in the background carries a shotgun while the man in the foreground has an M1 carbine fitted with a grenade-launching attachment on the barrel. (USMC)

Shotguns are simple weapons; easy to learn and use. They have been used in combat for centuries due to their close-range firepower. Modern use of the shotgun as an issued weapon really began during World War One.

Though never standard issue, the US Army issued them as needed for trench clearing, raids, and other close combat. Shotguns proved so effective in this role the German army protested their use and said they would execute any man who was captured with a shotgun. The United States promised reprisals if the Germans carried out their threats, so the latter came to nothing, but the value of the shotgun was demonstrated.

During World War Two the United States continued to issue shotguns, while other nations used them on a more ad hoc basis, if at all. In America shotguns were common hunting weapons, so there was wide expertise in their use. When the war began, the US shipped thousands of rifles to the UK as part of Lend-Lease, often stripping them from National Guard armouries. Many of these weapons were replaced with shotguns until new rifles became available.

Once America entered the war, shotguns went with its troops into the Pacific. In jungle fighting, enemy soldiers might only be seen for a second in the dense foliage. A quick shot with a shotgun loaded with buckshot had a higher probability of a hit than a rifle shot, though a .30-calibre bullet wound can be just as devastating. The spread of the buckshot gave a higher chance of a hit in such circumstances. US Army General Alexander Patch even carried a Winchester shotgun when leading a

LEFT: US Navy gunnery trainees learned how to lead aerial targets using shotguns. Note the large number of shell casings on the ground. (US NAVY)

For military use, shotguns typically had shortened barrels of 18 to 20ins and were frequently fitted with ventilated handguards and bayonet lugs. In this configuration they were often referred to as trench guns. Clay pigeons and full barrelled sporting shotguns were used to train anti-aircraft gunners and pilots in how to lead targets. Postwar studies showed this training was valuable for the pilots but did not seem to help the anti-aircraft gunners very much. The author has an old US Navy Remington Model 31 training shotgun and it is thoroughly worn out by the untold thousands of rounds put through it. It is a testament to the weapon's quality that it is still operational.

In combat, US troops used the venerable Winchester Model 1897, the Ithaca Model 37, Winchester Model 12, and various other types from manufacturers Remington and Stevens. These were all similar in operation, being pump-action designs. During the war, the United States purchased around a half a million shotguns of all types. A semi-automatic shotgun, the Browning Auto-5, saw use during the war, though details on its use are relatively scant. Made in Belgium, it likely saw use in several armies.

counterattack during the fighting on Guadalcanal.

Japanese snipers often hid in trees and foliage, so US troops would use shotguns to engage them. Even if the buckshot missed, it would shred the foliage, revealing their enemy's position. Marines used birdshot in their shotguns to bring down Japanese carrier pigeons.

BELOW: Two soldiers advance through machine gun fire at Bougainville, January 1944. The soldier on the left carries a Winchester Model 1897 shotgun, a holdover from World War One. (NARA)

Mortars

The infantry's portable artillery

RIGHT: A German mortar crew sets up their weapon in a crater next to a knocked-out T-34 tank, June 1942. Such a position provides good cover from return fire. (BUNDESARCHIV BILD 101I-218-0529-16)

BELOW: American soldiers of the 39th Infantry Regiment, 9th Infantry Division, prepare to fire a 60mm mortar from a very squarely dug mortar pit. Note the pine branches used to hide the excess soil. (NARA)

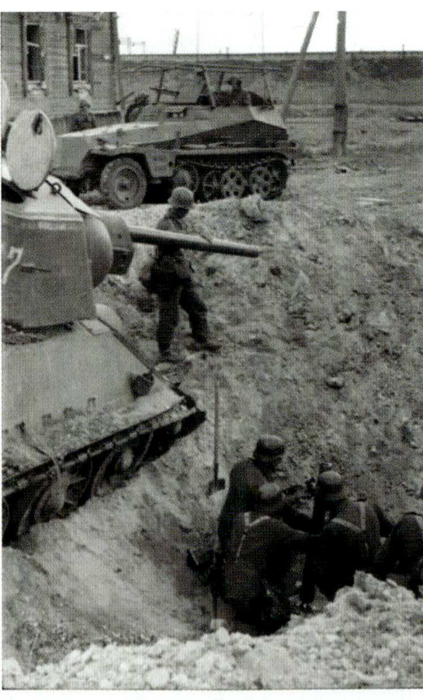

Prior to World War One, the term mortar applied to an artillery piece capable of high angle fire and generally used for sieges of towns and cities. They fell out of use with the advent of the more versatile howitzer, which also fired at a high angle. The trench warfare of World War One called for a portable weapon capable of launching projectiles toward enemy trenches and fortifications. Britain developed the Stokes mortar, which worked well for the purpose, and the French refined the design after the war. The modern mortar became a new weapon for the infantry.

The simple, cost-effective design meant mortars quickly proliferated throughout the world's armies. A mortar is essentially a metal tube enclosed on the bottom with a fixed firing pin. The tube is attached to a baseplate which spreads out the recoil, so the tube does not become buried in the ground after the first few rounds. The tube is usually supported by a bipod for stability, and has a sight which is aimed using a set of aiming stakes or by directly aiming at the target.

To fire, the mortar round is dropped down the tube where it strikes the firing pin, detonating the propellant and sending it towards the target. Mortar rounds are technically known as bombs, though the term is not always used. Most mortar tubes are smooth bore, though a few are rifled to impart a spin to the bomb, like a rifle bullet. Mortar bombs do not have to withstand the same firing pressure as artillery rounds, so they generally have thinner casings and can hold more explosives than a cannon round of the same size.

Compared to a cannon of the same calibre, mortars are lighter, making them portable by infantry. Most mortars could be broken down into the tube, bipod, baseplate and sight, with each member of the mortar crew carrying one of the components along with ammunition. The German army called their mortars Granatwerfer, or 'grenade launcher', and a few armies had small mortars which could fire modified hand grenades.

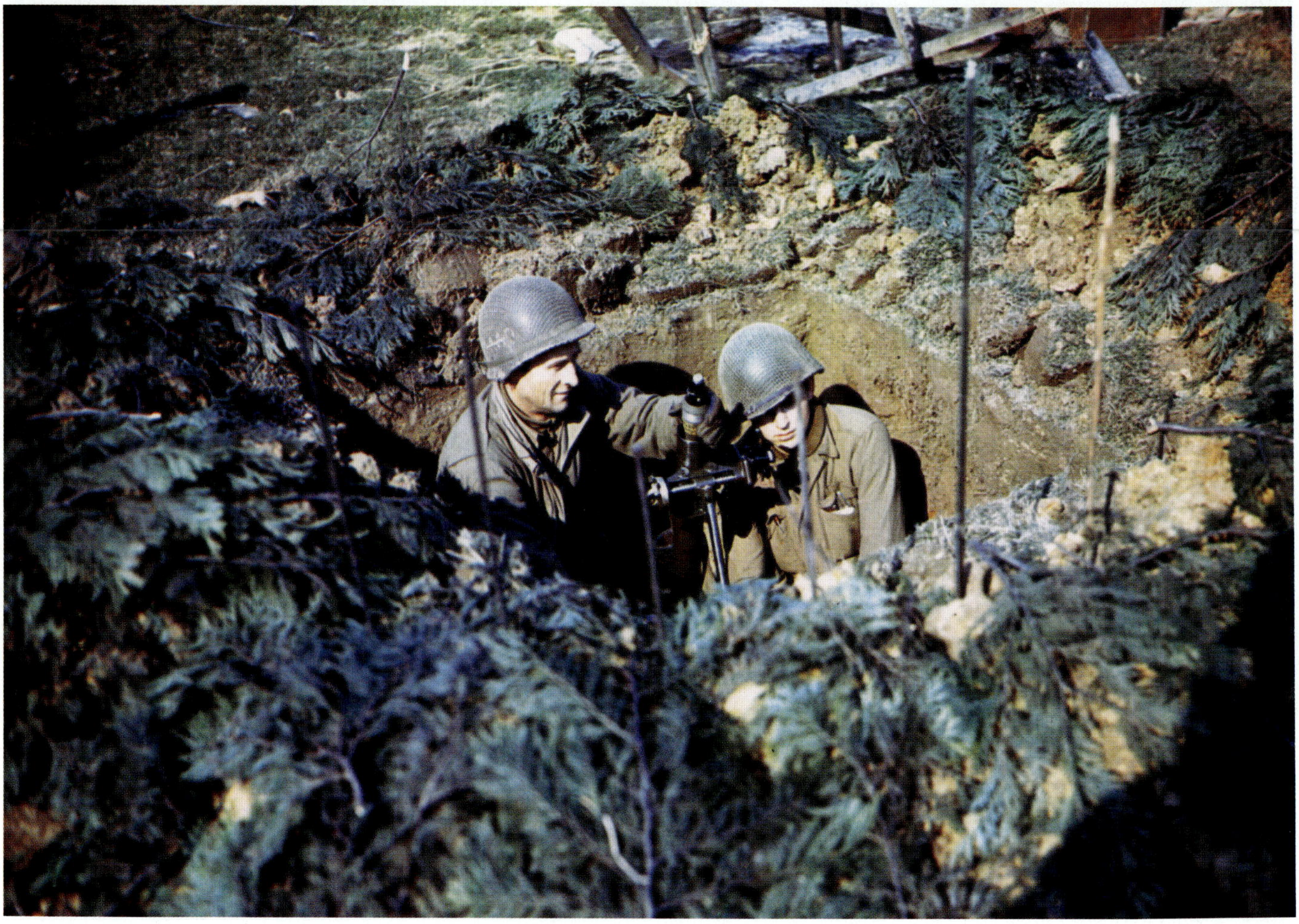

LEFT: Two Red Army 82mm mortars firing in the Carpathian Mountains, February 1945. These two weapons together could easily fire 50 rounds per minute for short periods. (RUSSIAN ARCHIVES)

Because they use a smaller propellant charge and fire only at a high angle, they have a shorter maximum range than artillery, making it necessary for infantry to keep them close to the fighting. Importantly, mortars have a high firing rate, sometimes up to 30 rounds per minute, although such a rate would eventually overheat the tube. The sustained firing rate on a cannon is usually around four rounds per minute, or less. This high rate of fire meant keeping mortars in action required steady ammunition resupply. If supply trucks were unavailable, soldiers in the unit might be given a round or two to carry. Bombs would be stockpiled near the tubes when the owning unit was in a static or defensive position. Mortars were versatile weapons, and most models could fire high-explosive or smoke rounds. Some smoke rounds contained white phosphorous, which could also start fires.

Lighter mortars, in the 50-60mm range, generally saw issue at the platoon or company level. Their light weight made them more easily portable for infantry companies. Most armies issued medium mortars, in the 80mm range, mostly at the battalion level. This could vary based on the nation in question and the type of infantry unit (standard, mechanised, or airborne).

Since they were in the company and battalion chain of command, mortars were often more responsive than artillery since they were closer and easier to contact. A fast barrage of several dozen mortar bombs could easily repel an attack or suppress an enemy position for a friendly attack.

Heavy Mortars. In this edition we focus on light and medium mortars, as they were an infantry weapon. However, heavier mortars existed and could be used for fire support. There were several notable models. The American M2 4.2inch (107mm) mortar earned the designation Chemical Mortar as it was used by the US Army Chemical Warfare Service for laying smoke screens. It also had a powerful high explosive round as well and were often used for fire support. The British developed a similar 4.2-inch weapon also issued to chemical warfare units, but it fired a useful explosive round as well, and was widely used.

The Soviet Union used two types of 120mm mortar, the M1938 and M1943, for fire support. Organised in batteries of four mortars for infantry support, they had the equivalent firepower of a 122mm howitzer with a higher rate of fire. The weapon proved so effective the Germans essentially copied it as the 12cm Granatwerfer 42.

BELOW: A 4.2-inch mortar crew fires at German tanks, February 1945. This tube is firing at a low angle to extend the range; note the sandbags piled on the baseplate and monopod front stand. The bombs appear to be smoke or white phosphorus rounds. (NARA)

Light Mortars

ABOVE: The crew of a Universal Carrier demonstrate how to use their 2in mortar in direct fire mode at Anzio, April 1944. (IWM NA13646)

Light mortars were usually the first available support weapon for frontline infantry. These weapons, generally in the 50-60mm range, served at the platoon and company level. Their small size and light weight made them portable, able to keep up with the infantry they supported. Their short range meant they had to stay close to the fighting, however, putting their crews at increased risk compared to the larger mortars, which could stay a few hundred yards further back.

Light mortars also tended to have high rates of fire. Their smaller bombs required less propellant, producing less heat and recoil on firing. This allowed more rounds to be fired before overheating became a problem.

As these bombs were smaller and less powerful, more might need to be fired to achieve good effects on target. Smaller bombs were less effective against field fortifications and bunkers, however, and would not destroy a well-made fortification, such as one of concrete. Despite this lack of

Light Mortars of World War II					
Nation	**Weapon**	**Calibre**	**Weight**	**ROF***	**Range**
UK	SMBL 2-inch	51mm	10.5lb (4.8kg)	8/12	500yds
US	M2	60mm	42lb (19kg)	18	1,900yds
France	M37	50mm	8lb (3.6kg)	20	503yds
Germany	GrW 36	50mm	31lb (14kg)	15/25	560yds
Japan	Type 89	50mm	10.6 lb (4.7kg)	25	700yds
Italy	Brixia M35	45mm	34lb (15.5kg)	8/10	580yds
Soviet Union	RM-38	50mm	27lb (12.1kg)	15/30	870yds
**RoF – Rate of Fire per minute Sustained/Maximum*					

explosive power, light mortars were still more powerful than any other weapon the infantry had on hand, and outranged their rifle grenades.

How these weapons were allocated depended on unit type. For example, a British infantry platoon had a 2-inch mortar in its platoon headquarters section. For an airborne platoon, the allocation was one per section, or three per platoon. A US Army rifle platoon had no mortars at the platoon level, but three 60mm M2 mortars in a weapons platoon at the company level. Each US airborne infantry platoon, however, had a 60mm mortar squad.

Notable light mortar models include:

British 2-inch mortar. This weapon possessed several unusual features. It had no bipod and a long, narrow baseplate. The user loaded it in the usual manner of dropping the round down the tube but it had a firing mechanism actuated by the user. The weapon had a sight, though skilled users could aim it by hand, even using it in a direct fire mode. The standard ammunition allocations totalled 36 rounds, a mix of smoke and high explosive rounds. Illumination and signalling rounds came in either red or green.

Japanese Type 89. Officially designated a grenade discharger, this small 50mm weapon bears the famous nickname 'knee mortar' which was given to it by Allied troops under the mistaken idea it was fired by bracing it against the knee. In actuality, doing so would cause injury, potentially even a broken femur. The Type 89 fired modified hand grenades or its own small bomb. These came in high explosive, illumination, and smoke variants. The weapon made a distinctive popping noise when fired; if fired close enough, Allied troops would hear it and have a few seconds to take cover. A Japanese platoon typically had three Type 89s.

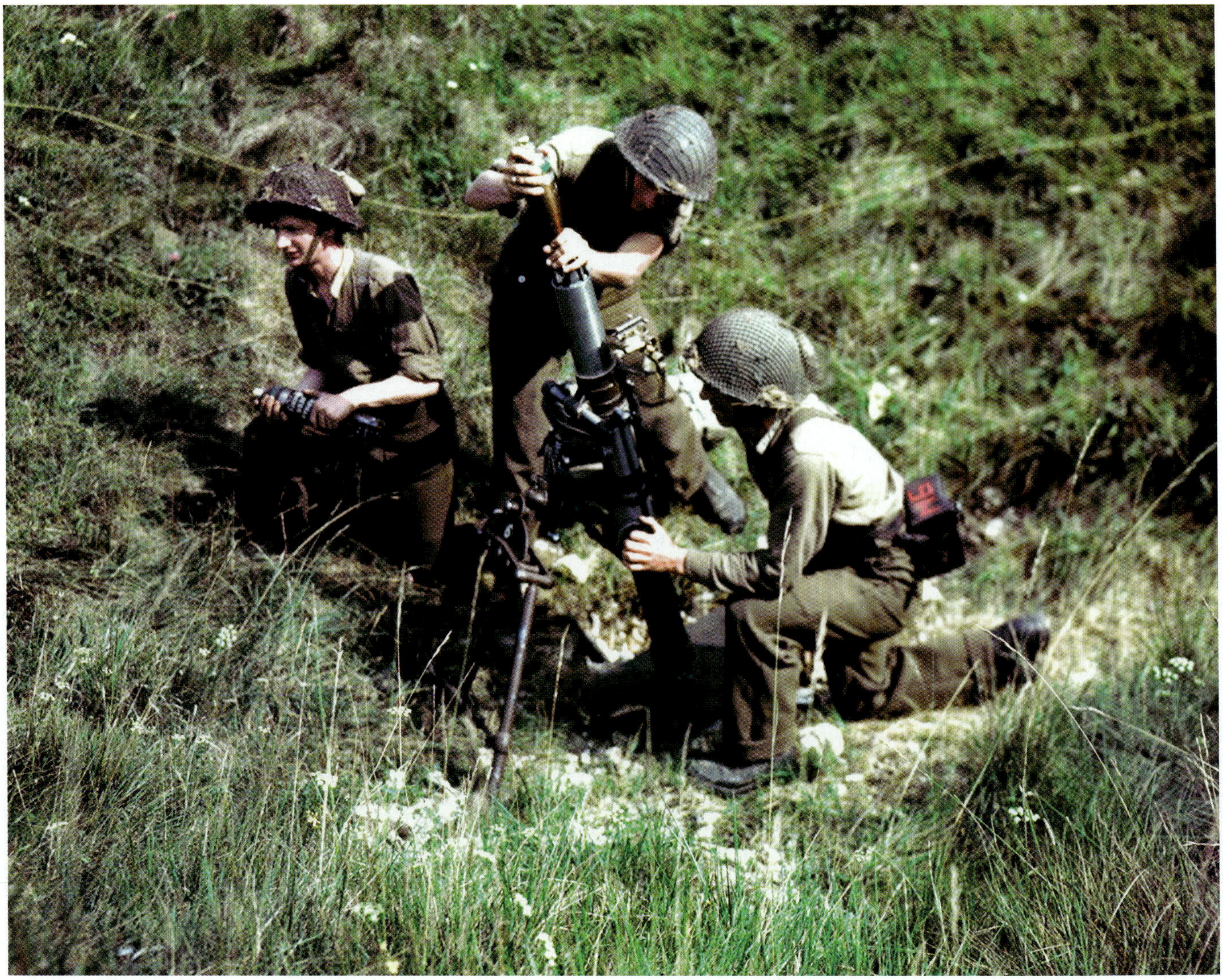

Medium Mortars

Portable and powerful

ABOVE: A Canadian 3-inch Mortar Team carry out a fire mission in France, 1944. These soldiers are wearing the late-war pattern 'turtle shell' helmet. (LIBRARY AND ARCHIVES CANADA)

RIGHT: Japanese Special Naval Landing Force troops prepare to fire their 81mm mortars at Buna-Gona in 1942. This is possible a drill since they are not wearing their helmets. (IJA JAPAN PUBLIC DOMAIN)

After the light mortars used at the platoon and company level, the infantry could next call on the support of the medium calibre mortars issued at the battalion and sometimes regimental level. These weapons had considerably more explosive power and longer range than the lighter mortars, enabling them to strike targets farther behind the front line, such as company or battalion command posts. Conversely, a commander could also place these longer-ranged mortars a little farther back from the fighting, making them harder to find and attack.

Most designs used by the major armies were 81mm weapons, with the Soviets using an 82mm calibre. There are stories that the Soviet

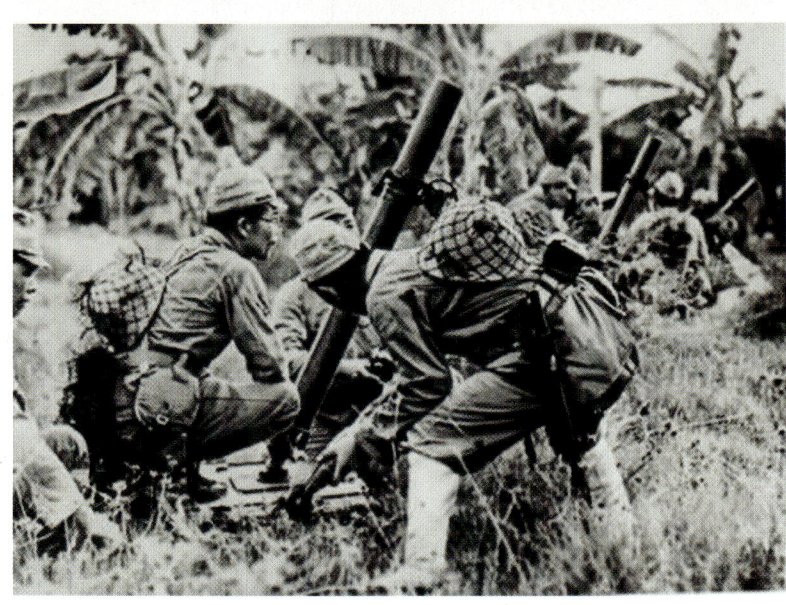

Medium Mortars of World War II					
Nation	Weapon	Calibre	Weight	ROF*	Range
UK	ML 3-inch	81mm	115.5lb (52.4kg)	12/25	2,800yds
US	M1	81mm	136lb (62kg)	18/35	3,300yds
France	Brandt M27/31	81mm	123lb (56kg)	18	3,000yds
Germany	GrW34	81.4mm	136.6lbs (62kg)	15/25	1,300yds
Japan	Type 97	81mm	145lbs (66kg)	15/20	3,000yds
Italy	81/14 M35	81mm	131lbs (60kg)	18	1,600yds**
Soviet Union	82.PM-41	82mm	123lb (56kg)	15/25	3,300yds

*RoF – Rate of Fire per minute Sustained/Maximum
The 81/14 M35 had a lightweight shell for long range fire, range 4,400yds

mortars were purposefully designed in 82mm so they could use captured ammunition while their opponents could not use the larger Soviet bombs. These claims are largely from the Cold War era, however. Some 81mm ammunition was interchangeable between nations; for example, Japanese ammunition would fire in US mortars, but with a reduction in range. Notably, the British ML 3-inch mortar was in 81mm, despite the 3-inch (76mm) designation.

A few armies, notably Japan and Germany, fielded mortars in the 90-100mm range, but these appear to be issued to artillery and specialised chemical warfare units, similar to the US and British 4.2-inch designs. Though not used by infantry, they were used in support of them with both smoke and high explosive bombs.

To get the most effect from mortar bombs, weapons crews used different fuses, as with larger cannon artillery. Light mortars used similar fuses, but we will discuss them here. Part of

a mortarman's training was in how to correctly set these fuses for each type of ammunition, including high-explosive, smoke, and illumination.

As an example, common US Army fuses included Point Detonating, which exploded on contact or with a very small (less than a second) delay. Concrete Piercing fuses were a delay fuse designed to let the bomb bury itself before exploding to cause more damage to fortifications. A thick concrete bunker would be able to withstand multiple hits from the relatively small 81mm mortar; however, such a fuse could be very effective against earth and wood construction. Mechanical Timing fuses could be set to explode a predetermined number of seconds after firing. Since time of flight for a given range was known and recorded in the weapon's firing manuals, this could achieve airburst detonations, which were much more deadly to exposed troops. The US developed a proximity fuse for mortars, but it entered service too late to see use during the war.

ABOVE LEFT: A drawing by a combat sketch artist of a German mortar squad in action. (NARA)

LEFT: The gunner of this US 81mm mortar crew is adjusting the weapon's aim while two others are stacking prepared mortar bombs for firing. (NARA)

LEFT: A 3-inch mortar crew of the British 20th Division firing a barrage near Prome, Burma, May 1945. Note the large number of bombs stacked and ready to fire. (IWM SE4041)

BELOW: A grainy image of a Red Army 82mm mortar emplaced on the outskirts of Moscow, December 1941. They have constructed overhead cover for their position using dirt over a wooden frame. With the mortar that low it will be difficult to aim precisely. (RIAN 60532)

Infantry Guns

Small cannon for infantry units

Friendly artillery is the infantryman's friend, when it is available. During World War Two field artillery units were typically controlled by higher headquarters at division or corps level, and there were always many demands for artillery fires beyond the direct support of infantry and combat units. Infantry units always wanted artillery support, but it was never guaranteed. To fill the gap between field artillery and the battalion and company mortars, some armies fielded light artillery pieces to infantry units at the battalion or regimental level.

These small guns provided a minimal artillery capability. The guns needed to be lightweight to ease transportation, and so usually had lightweight carriages and short barrels. The short barrels would reduce the velocity of the weapon's ammunition and reduce range. Since they were intended to give direct support to infantry units against field fortifications and similar targets, this was not considered a disadvantage. Most designs had a gun shield to protect the crew since they would often fire directly at their target from short ranges.

Small field guns were not a new concept in World War Two and a few armies were issuing them before the war. The Japanese Army, for example, issued two Type 92 70mm guns to

LEFT: Chinese soldiers man a captured Japanese Type 92 infantry gun. While a posed image, it does show the gun, along with its equipment and ammunition. (CHINESE ARCHIVES PUBLIC DOMAIN)

BOTTOM: This Japanese Type 92 70mm gun was captured by US Marines on Saipan and turned against its owners at the town of Garapan. (NARA)

BELOW: American soldiers of the 101st Infantry Regiment clean their 105mm pack howitzer, part of the regimental cannon company, October 1944. (NARA)

Typical Infantry Guns of World War II					
Nation	Model	Calibre	Weight	RoF*	Range
United States	M3	105mm	2,495lb (1130kg)	2/4	8,300yds
Germany	Le. IG 18	75mm	882lb (400kg)	8/12	3,880yds
Germany	sIG 33	150mm	4,000lb (1,800kg)	2/3	5,100yds
Japan	Type 92	70mm	476lbs (216kg)	10	3,000yds
Soviet Union	M1943	76mm	1,322lbs (600kg)	10/12	4,500yds
*Rate of Fire is Sustained/Maximum if known					

each infantry battalion, leading to the weapons' designation as a 'Battalion Gun'. It used typical high explosive rounds but also had a shaped charge anti-tank round.

The German Army issued infantry guns, called Infanteriegeschütz, or simply IG, from the early 1930s. Most came in 75mm calibre, but Germany did field the largest infantry gun used during the war – the sIG 33 150mm weapon. It used high explosive, smoke and an anti-tank round. A specialised 300mm demolition round for destroying fortifications and obstacles fitted over the muzzle and held 119lb (54kg) of explosives. This gun was also mounted on an obsolete tank chassis to make a self-propelled weapon.

The Soviet Army used artillery of all types extensively as part of its doctrine. It issued 76mm guns to infantry regiments from the late 1920s. Red Army troops began the war with the M1927, which was improved into the M1943 mid-war.

Both guns served until war's end and were overall similar.

The US Army never fielded a dedicated infantry gun, instead creating the M3 105mm light howitzer. This weapon went to airborne field artillery battalions alongside the 75mm pack howitzer. Each American infantry regiment had a cannon company, and these were officially issued with six M3 howitzers. It used the same projectiles and cases as the larger 105mm cannon, but had its own propellant charges to avoid unburnt powder leaving the muzzle due to the shorter barrel. The author interviewed a veteran of the cannon company of the US 157th Infantry Regiment, who stated his unit used M7 105mm self-propelled guns in the last months of the war. This indicates American infantry regiments may have acquired or been issued other types of artillery in an ad hoc manner, based on need or weapons availability.

Anti-Tank Weapons

lighter, as they only needed to be able to penetrate 15-25mm of armour protection.

Many nations produced Anti-Tank (AT) rifles as an adequate solution. Although they were heavy, AT rifles could be transported easily enough by two or three soldiers. AT rifles did not work out as well as hoped, and tank armour quickly became thicker to defeat them and the existing AT guns, which were generally in the 25-40mm range. Much of the problem was due to the use of solid shot, which lacked an explosive charge to cause damage after penetration. This was particularly problematic with AT rifles, whose small projectiles lacked space for a useful explosive charge or the power to do much damage after a successful penetration.

The shaped charge warhead vastly increased the penetrating power of AT weapons light enough for infantry use. A shaped charge weapon focused its explosive force

ABOVE: A US bazooka team fires on a Panther tank. This is a posed shot, as the tank appears previously knocked out, but the image shows the blast and smoke effect of a hit. (NARA)

"The best weapon against a tank is another tank," is a common saying among military experts. There is certainly truth in this statement. However, tanks are not always available, may not be where they are needed, and some World War Two armies simply could not afford them at the scale required. Infantry is the major combat force in any army, so specialised anti-tank weapons became vital for them.

Tanks evolved rapidly during the war. At the beginning, tanks were relatively small with thin armour, proof more against small arms fire and artillery shrapnel. Accordingly, infantry anti-tank weapons were also smaller and

in a particular direction to increase armour penetration; importantly, the shaped charge did not depend on high velocity to achieve this.

By late 1942, the American M1 2.36-inch rocket launcher (commonly called the bazooka) entered combat in North Africa and proved effective against German and Italian armoured vehicles. The British Projector, Infantry, Anti-Tank (PIAT) also used a shaped charge warhead but a different launching mechanism.

German troops captured examples of the M1 Bazooka sent to the Soviets and used on the Eastern Front. These went back to Germany for evaluation and more were captured from American forces in Tunisia. The Germans made some improvements, most critically using a larger rocket, and put it into service as the Panzerschreck. A one-shot disposable weapon called the Panzerfaust also proved very effective.

The combatant nations created all these weapons as part of the ongoing race to keep up with the growing size and armour protection of tanks, mainly those of the Soviet and German armies on the Eastern Front. The length and scope of the campaign on that front forced such competition. The Western Allies did not have the same pressure due to their having to fight the Germans for shorter time periods on different fronts. However, what the Germans produced for the Eastern Front also saw service in the West, so weapons like the bazooka and PIAT did not keep pace with the latest enemy developments.

Infantry also used mines (often laid by engineers) and anti-tank grenades of various types. Some AT grenades were fired from rifles while others required a soldier to approach the tank and physically attach the weapon or throw it from close range. Mines were best used when laid as part of an integrated defence, where minefields were covered by AT guns or other weapons, which engaged when the enemy tanks had to stop for the minefield. Most AT mines could disable a tank by breaking its track, though some larger types could also damage the tank itself. Most designs would only detonate under the weight of an armoured vehicle and would fail to explode if a soldier stepped on it.

As a last resort, infantry used Molotov cocktails – a bottle of petrol with a rag for a wick – or demolition charges at close range. Sometimes multiple grenades would be fastened together and thrown onto the engine deck or jammed under the turret's overhang. This took courage on the part of the attacking soldier, although tanks have poor visibility of the area immediately surrounding the vehicle if the crew hatches are

all shut. Japanese troops used such tactics more often as they possessed fewer AT guns. Such close attacks also fit well with the Japanese practice of close combat, though in practice such close attacks were very costly in terms of casualties.

Whatever weapons were available, infantry frequently formed tank hunting teams, particularly in close or urban terrain where it was easier to get close to a tank unobserved. Experienced tank units worked closely with infantry in such terrain to keep this threat at a distance. The tank hunting teams would use artillery and mortar fire to separate the enemy tanks from their supporting infantry.

ABOVE: Three American soldiers pose with a captured German T-Gewehr anti-tank rifle. This First World War weapon saw limited service in 1939-45. (NARA)

BELOW LEFT: A Finnish soldier aims a Panzerfaust while another covers him with a Suomi submachine gun. (SA-KUVA)

BELOW: A German soldier receives the 'tank destruction badge'. A silver badge indicated one enemy tank destroyed while a gold badge signified five tanks destroyed. (BUNDESARCHIV)

Boys Anti-Tank Rifle

The Boys Mark I series of anti-tank rifles saw wide service with the Western Allies during the first three years of the war. It was named after Captain HC Boys, the Assistant Superintendent of Design at the Royal Small Arms Factory in Enfield. He led the development effort on the weapon, which was originally called the Stanchion. Tragically he died shortly before its adoption by the British Army, so it was renamed in his honour.

The Boys (often misspelled 'Boyes') used a top loading magazine for its .55 calibre round, which was based on the American .50 calibre machine gun cartridge. The sights were offset to the left as a result. The rifle used a T-shaped monopod instead of the more common bipod. It used a muzzle brake and a recoiling barrel mechanism to reduce the recoil felt by the firer, though the Boys was known among users for its brutal recoil.

RIGHT: A Chevrolet truck of the Long Range Desert Group in North Africa, March 1941. The gunner in the rear has a Boys, which would be effective against enemy trucks, armoured cars or most things short of a tank. (IWM E2298)

RIGHT: British troops on the march in France 1940, two men carrying a Boys. German tanks were up armoured after Poland, making the Boys even less effective against them. (IWM 0758)

so each rifle platoon had one in its headquarters section. Boys were fitted on the Universal Carrier (often called the Bren Carrier), so a mechanised platoon would have four. The Soviets received about 3,200 of them, likely along with a similar number of Universal Carriers sent as aid.

The Boys saw its first combat use in Finland during the Winter War, but the British Expeditionary Force used it in Norway, Belgium and France soon after in 1940. They were mostly ineffective against the frontal armour of the German tanks. A shot at the side or rear armour had a better chance of penetration. One account from North Africa stated the Boys was too heavy and so was normally given to the company drunk as a punishment. The Canadians used them at Dieppe in August 1942 as a long-range sniping weapon.

The US Marine Raiders used them successfully as a weapon against light or unarmoured targets. During the Makin Island Raid in August 1942, the Raiders used the Boys on two Japanese seaplanes. One caught fire and the other was so badly damaged it crashed when the pilot attempted to escape.

Factories in the UK and Canada produced the Boys, making over 113,000 of them before production ended in December 1943. Six thousand went to the Chinese army while 700 were supplied to the United States and issued to the US Army Rangers and the Marine Raiders. British and Commonwealth service units issued them down to the company level,

Boys Mark I Anti-Tank Rifle	
Calibre	.55-calibre (13.9mm)
Magazine	5-round detachable box
Length	62in (1.57m)
Weight	35lb (16kg)
Rate of Fire	10 rpm
Penetration	23mm at 100yds

German Anti-Tank Rifles

Early war tank busters

Germany developed the anti-tank rifle during the First World War to give infantry a minimal defence against armoured vehicles. Field guns in direct fire were the preferred weapon, with anti-tank rifles used to fill the gaps between the artillery pieces. The first anti-tank rifle, adopted in January 1918, was the tankgewehr, or tank rifle, usually shortened to T-Gewehr. It fired a 13mm steel-core bullet with a massive powder charge to give it more velocity and penetrating power. Some of these served during World War II and were captured by Allied troops.

Before World War II Germany developed two anti-tank rifles, designated Panzerbüsche (PzB). The PzB38 proved too complex for effective mass production and was discontinued in favour of the simpler PzB39, which both fired the same 7.92x94mm round. Curiously, this ammunition had a small ampule of tear gas in the projectile. Once the steel-core round penetrated the tank, the tear gas was supposed to force them to abandon their vehicle. However, Allied experience showed the tear gas was insufficient to force the crew out of the tank, and often the ampule separated from the projectile when it struck the armour plate and remained outside the tank.

German factories produced just over 40,000 anti-tank rifles of both types before production ceased in 1941. The ammunition stayed in production until 1942 with 9.4 million rounds made. The German military also adopted a few thousand Czech-made anti-tank rifles but these saw limited use as by then the anti-tank rifle was obsolete. About 28,000 PzB39s were converted to grenade launchers designated as GrB39. This could fire the standard rifle grenades from the Mauser 98K, with two types of anti-tank grenades and one anti-personnel grenade available. The GrB39 served until the end of the war.

Despite their ineffectiveness against tanks, these anti-tank rifles continued in service even during the invasion of the Soviet Union. German troops had more success using them against Soviet light tanks and armoured cars. They were also effective as a long-range weapon against troops or for shooting through walls and into bunkers made of timber or sandbags. German AT rifles stayed in service until the end of the war as an ad hoc weapon, issued to Volkssturm militia and others due to weapons shortages in the last months of the war. The Panzerfaust and Panzerschreck replaced them as a frontline weapon.

ABOVE: Two German soldiers man a strongpoint near a road in Russia in Autumn 1941. They have an MG34 machine gun and a PzB39. (BUNDESARCHIV_BILD_101I-771-0382-07A)

LEFT: A German soldier carries his anti-tank rifle in the Libyan desert, April 1941. (BUNDESARCHIV_BILD_101I-783-0123-27A)

German Anti-tank Rifles

	T-Gewehr	PzB39
Calibre	13.2mm	7.92x94mm
Feed	Single shot	Single shot
Length	67in (1.69m)	63.8in (1,62m)
Weight	41lb (18.5kg)	27.8lb (12.6kg)
Penetration	26mm at 100yds	25mm at 300yds

Soviet Anti-Tank Rifles

The most widely used AT rifles of the war

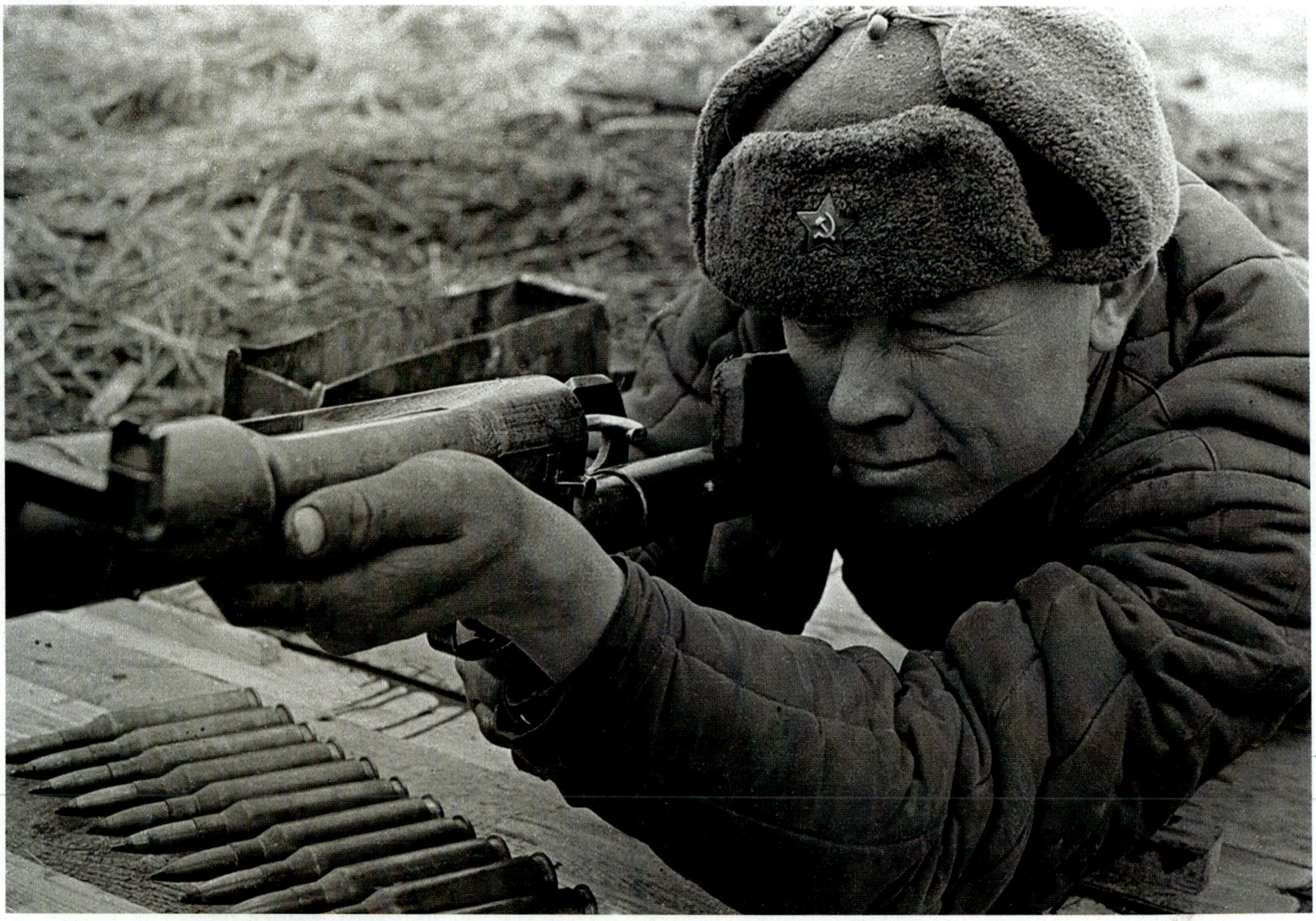

ABOVE: A PTRD gunner tales aim on the Kalinin Front, 1942. He has 11 14.5mm rounds laid out for quick reloading. (MOSCOW ARCHIVES)

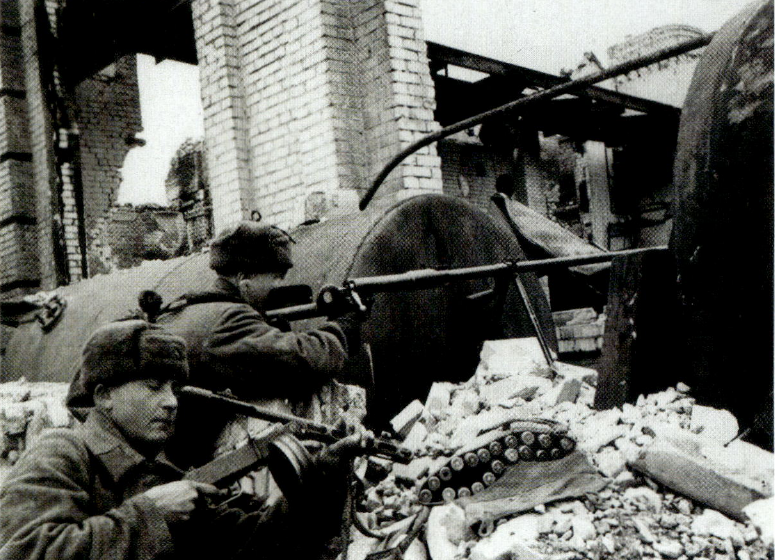

RIGHT: A PTRD gunner of the 108th Guards Rifle Regiment, 36th Guards Rifle Division, takes aim at Stalingrad, November 1942. The ammunition bag for the PTRD is in front of the assistant's submachine gun. (RUSSIAN ARCHIVES)

The Red Army adopted anti-tank rifles in the 1930s after a series of experiments. The weapon designs were inadequate, but the testing succeeded in creating a useful 14.5mm cartridge. This cartridge had a considerable propellant charge, giving it substantially more power and penetration than the AT rifles developed elsewhere. The projectiles also carried a small incendiary charge to create damage after penetration. One drawback of the AT rifles was the inability of the projectile to cause crippling damage after it penetrated the armour, often requiring multiple hits.

Several different weapons saw limited production, including a copy of the German T-Gewehr chambered for the

Soviet Anti-tank Rifles		
	PTRD	**PTRS**
Calibre	14.5mm	14.5mm
Magazine	Single shot	5-round detachable box
Length	79.5in (2.02m)	83in (2.1m)
Weight	38lb (17.3kg)	46lb (21kg)
Rate of Fire	8-10rpm	10-15rpm
Penetration	34mm at 500yds	34mm at 500yds

Soviet 12.7mm round. After creating the 14.5mm ammunition, however, the Soviets sharply curtailed their AT rifle program in 1940, partly due to technical problems. The adoption of other AT weapons such as light anti-tank guns also eclipsed existing AT rifle designs.

Once the war with Germany began, the Soviets embarked on several crash weapons programs, including AT rifles, once field experience showed the lighter and older German panzers were vulnerable to their fire. They first reverse-engineered captured examples of the German PzB39, but production halted after 426 were made when the town where the factory was located came under German siege during October 1941.

Two new models quickly entered development to fill the gap. Both used the 14.5mm cartridge. To produce usable weapons in the shortest possible time, the Soviets assigned two experienced weapons designers, Degtyaryev and Simonov, both of whom already had successful weapon designs in Soviet service.

Degtyaryev's creation went into production in October 1941 and saw combat use in the defence of Moscow. Designated the PTRD, it was a single-shot, bolt-action weapon. As it had no recoil mechanism or magazine, the PTRD was simple to make, rugged and reliable in service. From 1941 to 1944, several factories produced 281,000 PTRDs.

Simonov produced a semi-automatic AT rifle called the PTRS. It used a five round magazine and was fitted with an adjustable gas regulator to help keep the weapon firing in extremely cold weather or when dirty. Over 190,000 PTRS rifles were built, and 14.5mm ammunition production amounted to almost 140 million rounds by 1945.

Troops liked both weapons, although many preferred the rugged and simple PTRD. The main reason for this preference centred on the tendency of the PTRS to start jamming after about 10-15 rounds. The PTRD had a lower rate of fire, but troops prized its reliability more.

In action, both weapons were more effective against the side or rear armour of tanks, particularly as tank armour improved over the course of the war. One German assault gun crewman reported his vehicle being hit by over ten rounds from an AT rifle, but only three penetrated the side skirt armour and had no energy left afterwards to do damage. This German also noted that the low profile of an AT rifle crew firing from the prone meant the German crew never saw the Soviet troops and did not even know they were attacked until later. A Soviet sergeant said in an interview: "I can see it but it can't see me. My rifle is small and hard to hit, but it can't see me."

In action, Soviet gunners would swarm German tanks, concentrating multiple AT rifles against one tank. German crews noted that when this happened, all the tank's vision blocks would be shot out within minutes. Afterwards the Soviets would move to secondary positions. AT rifles also saw use against lighter vehicles, bunkers, and artillery pieces. Partisans reported them as very effective against railroad locomotives, using them to destroy the boilers.

At Kursk and elsewhere, the Soviets integrated AT rifles into their anti-tank defence plans. Interspersed with anti-tank guns, the AT rifles covered obstacles such as minefields and anti-tank ditches. From cover they could place fire on any armoured vehicles which had to stop, and any combat engineers who tried to breach the obstacles.

However innovative their use, the PTRD and PTRS were always of limited use against panzers but could be very effective against most other targets. After the war these AT rifles saw service in the Korean War, given as aid to North Korea. Like many Soviet-era weapons, they are still seen on battlefields in Ukraine.

LEFT: A Soviet PTRD crew in a defensive position outside Moscow, December 1941. At close range the PTRD was dangerous to any German tank then in service. (ZELENOGRAD MUSEUM)

BELOW: A Red Army soldier fires his PTRS from a ruined building in the North Caucasus in late 1942. His assistant provides cover with a PPSH41 submachine gun. (RUSSIAN MOD)

Anti-Tank Grenades and Charges

Handheld anti-tank weapons

RIGHT: A factory worker assembling No. 74 Sticky Bombs in 1943. The weapon came with a five second fuze. (IWM D14772)

The infantry always had to fear the appearance of tanks and armoured vehicles on the battlefield. Whenever possible infantrymen wanted their own armour and anti-tank guns working with them to provide supporting firepower, and to defend them against any enemy tanks which appeared. However, sometimes no support was available, and troops had to act without it. Airborne troops could not take armour with them, having only light anti-tank and field guns along, dropped by parachute or in gliders. This problem was especially acute early in the war before the advent of weapons such as the PIAT or bazooka.

To give troops some hope of defending themselves, most armies developed handheld anti-tank (AT) weapons. For this discussion, handheld refers to weapons which are thrown or placed by hand rather than fired. These weapons were generally small explosive devices, sometimes purpose-designed and other times developed from hand grenades

BELOW: A group of Japanese soldiers use petrol bombs on a British M3 Stuart tank in Burma. This is a posed or training photograph, as the tank appears to have already been knocked out and is missing its left track. (IJA JAPAN PUBLIC DOMAIN)

or engineer demolition charges. Early in the war tanks had thinner armour and so handheld weapons could be more effective. Later in the war, thicker armour and larger tanks made handheld weapons an even more desperate measure.

Handheld weapons were tactically difficult to use as they required soldiers to approach the tank or otherwise be very close to it. The challenge here is that tanks rarely operate alone. They usually operate in groups, enabling tanks to cover each other with fire against approaching infantry. Accounts from American tank crews in the Pacific note having to spray each other's tanks down with machine gun fire when Japanese infantry tried to swarm over them. Further, veteran tank crews prefer to operate with infantry support, so that the tanks protect the infantry against threats such as machine gun nests while the infantry deal with AT guns and prevent enemy infantry from getting too close. Infantry defending against a tank attack used machine guns, mortars and artillery to separate tanks and infantry, leaving the tanks vulnerable to close attack.

Many handheld AT weapons appeared during the war, issued by various armies. Below are some of the most notable and interesting ones. See page 78 for anti-tank rifle grenades.

Panzerknacker. Officially named the Hafthohlladung, or 'adhesive hollow charge,' this shaped charge weapon used three magnets to attach to an enemy tank, requiring the soldier to move up to the tank to attach it. The magnets also provided the proper distance for the charge to function correctly. After emplacing it, the user pulled an igniter atop the mine and retreated out of the blast area. If seated correctly, it could penetrate an impressive 140mm of armour. Its fuze provided 4.5 or 7.5 seconds before detonation, depending on variant. The Germans produced over 550,000 before replacing it with the Panzerfaust. A hand-thrown shaped charge grenade, the Panzerwurfmine, proved less successful.

Sticky Bomb. Officially the No.74 grenade, this unusual weapon consisted of a glass sphere filled with 560 grams of explosive and wrapped in a cloth sock-like netting which was covered in an adhesive. A thin metal case enclosed the sphere with the weapon's handle protruding from the bottom. The user removed the metal case, pulled a pin on the handle, and then threw the grenade, which would ideally stick to the target and explode.

Shitotsubakurai Lunge Mine. This shaped charge weapon first saw combat in the Philippines in December 1944. It consisted of a warhead attached to a 6-7ft-long pole. Three metal legs attached to the warhead ensured the correct distance for warhead function. Essentially a suicide weapon, the user had to remove the safety pin, charge the tank and strike its armour, preferably at a 90° angle. When the legs hit the tank, the pole was pushed forward, causing the weapon to explode, also killing the user. If deployed properly, it could penetrate up to 150mm of armour.

The Japanese deployed another AT weapon called the hook charge, an explosive charge which could be attached to the tank's cannon barrel to disable it. They also used a hand grenade with an impact fuze called the Hand Mine. It was simply a spherical bomb holding 3lb of explosives.

Improvised Weapons. Soldiers used their ingenuity to use other devices against tanks. AT mines could be attached to a rope and pulled across a trail or road in front of a tank as it moved. Once the tank was close, the crew would not be able to see the mine being pulled into view. This technique appears in field manuals of the period. The petrol bomb, popularly known as the Molotov cocktail, saw frequent use, particularly in built-up areas where soldiers could easily get close enough to throw them or drop them from the upper storeys of buildings. If thrown onto the engine deck of a tank, the burning petrol could drip down into the engine compartment and destroy belts and hoses.

ABOVE: A Royal Engineer holds a Panzerknacker magnetic mine. If allowed to get close, a German soldier could knock out a tank by placing it on the side or rear armour. (IWM B6015)

LEFT: A drawing from a wartime US Army bulletin shows how a Japanese soldier employed the Lunge Mine, though at the cost of his own life. (NARA)

PIAT

British anti-tank weapon

The Projector, Infantry, Anti-Tank, known by the acronym PIAT, served British and Commonwealth forces as their basic infantry anti-tank (AT) weapon. It fulfilled the same role as the bazooka and Panzerschreck. Like those weapons, the PIAT came about from the effort to create a more effective AT weapon for infantry than the AT rifle. It entered service in early 1943 in Tunisia, North Africa.

The PIAT operated on the concept of a spigot mortar. The design takes a solid rod (the spigot) fixed within a short tube. In the PIAT the spigot is attached to a heavy spring and when it is fired the spigot is pushed forward into the base of the ammunition, a rocket with a shaped charge warhead. This rocket had a propellant charge in its tail which was ignited by the spigot. The PIAT had a tray-like area at the front of the tube for holding the projectile and a shoulder pad to cushion recoil when firing.

The weapon had to be cocked before firing. To do so, the user had to place their feet on the shoulder pad, rotate the body of the PIAT one quarter-turn to unlock it and then pull the body up until the spring was locked into place by the trigger sear. Now cocked, the PIAT's body could then be lowered, turned back a quarter-turn, and locked into place again. This could be very difficult for soldiers who had to lay prone due to enemy fire or for short-statured soldiers.

In use, soldiers cocked the weapon when not in action and carried their PIAT around that way until it was needed. Then, the assistant could put a round of ammunition in the tray and the weapon would quickly be ready to fire. When the soldier did fire the PIAT, the spigot went into the rocket's tail, igniting the propellent and launching the rocket at its target. The exploding propellant pushed the spigot and spring back down, re-cocking it for the next shot. This made the weapon easier to use after the first shot, since it now only needed to be reloaded.

Since shaped charge weapons do not depend on the velocity of the projectile for their armour-piercing power, it was perfect for the PIAT, which launched projectiles at a relatively slow 240 to 450ft per second. It could penetrate

PIAT	
Calibre	83mm
Length	39in (99cm)
Weight	32lb (15kg)
Effective Range	115yds (105m)
Penetration	4in (102mm)

LEFT: After cocking, the PIAT was reloaded by laying a new round of ammunition in the tray at the weapon's front. (NARA)

up to 4ins of armour, though in action this number proved hard to achieve due to the PIAT's poor accuracy and problems with the ammunition. The weapon's harsh recoil made it difficult to use effectively. The official effective range of the PIAT stood at 115yds, with a maximum range of 350yds, using it as an indirect fire weapon similar to a mortar. Many users considered it good only to 50yds or so.

Sgt Charles 'Wagger' Thornton served as a para in the Oxford and Buckinghamshire Light Infantry during the Normandy landings, when his company conducted a glider assault of two bridges over the Orne River and Caen Canal. He held a low opinion of the PIAT, saying "The PIAT is actually a load of rubbish, really. The range is around about 50yds and no more. You're a dead loss if you try to go farther."

Despite his dislike of the PIAT, Thornton employed a PIAT to effectively save his company's position at the bridges. When a Panzer IV approached the bridge in advance of a large German force, Thornton hid in a pile of rubbish and waited until the tank stood only 30yds away. He fired a single shot which destroyed the tank and blocked the advance of the rest of the German force. Another para used a PIAT to destroy a German patrol boat that approached the bridges later that day.

Several soldiers earned a Victoria Cross for determined use of the PIAT.

In May 1944, L Cpl Francis Jefferson of the Lancashire Fusiliers used a PIAT during the fighting around Monte Cassino. When his position came under German attack by two German Sturmgeschutz assault guns, he advanced under enemy fire and fired his PIAT from the hip, destroying the lead vehicle. The recoil knocked him over, but he reloaded and prepared to engage a second vehicle, though its crew retreated before he could fire.

In June 1944, Gurkha rifleman Ganju Lama used a PIAT at Imphal.

When Japanese tanks counterattacked against his unit, he crawled to within 30yds of the lead tank, suffering three wounds along the way. His first shot destroyed the tank, so Ganju Lama turned his PIAT against the second, destroying it as well. While a nearby anti-tank gun destroyed the last tank, the young Gurkha attacked the crews of the tanks as they tried to escape, killing several of them and wounding more. Both soldiers earned the Victoria Cross for their courage under fire.

BELOW: A British soldier fires his PIAT in Normandy, August 1944. The PIAT could jump when fired; the cloth is likely to keep dust from being raised. (IWM B8355)

M1 and M9 Bazooka

The answer seemed to be in the shaped charge, an explosive warhead designed to direct the initial power of its explosive charge in one direction, greatly increasing armour penetration. Rifle grenades were developed using this technology, but they were limited in range by the weight and size of the warhead, making a truly effective AT grenade too large to be fired from a rifle.

A team of Army engineers took this shaped charge warhead and mated it to a rocket motor. According to one of the designers, Edward Uhl, he was thinking of how to launch his rocket

Virtually every hand-held anti-tank rocket launcher traces its heritage to the M1 2.36in rocket launcher, commonly known as the 'bazooka'. That nickname derived from a novelty musical instrument created and played by Bob Burns, a comedian of the 1930s, familiar to American soldiers of the period. That name became so ubiquitous that bazooka is now a generic term for any hand-held, shoulder fired rocket launcher.

The M1 came from the US Army's search for an effective and lightweight anti-tank (AT) weapon for infantry use. As the Americans watched the fighting in Europe, they noted the limitations of existing infantry AT weapons, such as the AT rifle and various grenades. Tanks were also quickly growing in size, and had thicker armour. They were quickly becoming invulnerable to the current crop of small AT weapons.

RIGHT: US Marines on Peleliu use a bazooka to blast Japanese snipers at a safe distance. (USMC)

BELOW: A bazooka team look on as a Panther tank burns. This image was most likely posed, or taken shortly after the action, as the photographer is directly in the path of the weapon's backblast. (NARA)

projectile when he walked past a pile of rubbish which had a pipe about the same diameter as his rocket. He realised he could put the rocket in the tube and fire it from the shoulder. The Army tested the crude prototype against other weapons under testing, and it was the only one which reliably hit the target eight of nine times. The M1 Bazooka was born.

The Army rushed the weapon into production with an initial order for 5,000. This first run went to the British and Soviets under Lend-Lease. The British tested them in North Africa and found the range too short for use in the open desert, so they were not issued. The Soviets said the bazooka was too inaccurate, underpowered, and the backblast revealed the shooter's position. They continued to use their AT rifles. They did send a few into combat, however and these were the first ones captured by the Germans.

The Americans took bazookas with them to North Africa, but the troops knew nothing about them. A few officers found them in their packing crates, figured out how to use them and began training soldiers. Two of the first uses of the weapon by Americans were against Vichy French forces. One soldier used a bazooka to shoot the rear entrance of a Vichy French coastal defence emplacement, causing its commander to immediately surrender. Another soldier fired one at a Vichy French tank column and struck a tree. This made the French commander think they were under artillery fire, so he also surrendered.

During the invasion of Sicily, paratroopers used the bazooka in tank-hunting teams, though the weapon also proved effective in attacking

bunkers and fortifications. The 505th Parachute Infantry Regiment had local nuns sew 'bazooka patches' which were given to soldiers who had knocked out a tank with their weapon. By mid-1943 an improved model, the M1A1, entered production. This model had several improvements to simplify the weapon and its manufacture.

Within a few months the M9 bazooka entered service. This version used a magneto for igniting the rockets rather than a battery. It could be disassembled for easier carrying, and fire improved rockets which could penetrate an additional inch of armour. White Phosphorus rockets were also available. The later M9A1

incorporated an optical sight instead of the standard iron sights.

When handled well by aggressive troops, bazookas could be decisive weapons. In May 1944, Sgt Van Barfoot led a platoon in the 157th Infantry Regiment. In combat near Carano, Italy, the platoon became pinned down by a strongly defended German position. He went forward alone, toward the enemy's left flank. He destroyed one enemy machine gun nest with a grenade and moved to the next one, killing two Germans with his Thompson submachine gun and capturing three more. A third German machine gun crew simply surrendered to him. After seizing the position and consolidating on it, the Germans launched a counterattack with three Tiger tanks. Taking up a bazooka, Barfoot blew the track off the first one at 75 yards. The other two Tigers withdrew towards a flank. Barfoot killed three of the disabled tank's crew with his Thompson as they abandoned their vehicle. For his actions that day, Barfoot received a Medal of Honor. He was later commissioned, and retired from the army as a colonel.

ABOVE: These GIs have cleverly mounted two bazookas on the machine gun mount of a jeep. Note the improvised armour on the vehicle. (NARA)

LEFT: A paratrooper uses a bazooka against a Japanese bunker on Corregidor, February 1945. The dust behind him indicates he has just fired. (NARA)

US Anti-tank rocket launchers		
	M1	**M9**
Calibre	2.36in (60mm)	2.36in (60mm)
Length	54in (1.4m)	61in (1.5m)
Weight	18lb (8.2kg) unloaded	15.1lb (6.87kg)
Effective Range	150yds (140m)	150yds (140m)
Penetration	Up to 3in (76mm)	Up to 4in (102mm)

ABOVE: German troops prepare to fire at a target on the Eastern Front, March 1944. Both soldiers are wearing their gas masks to protect against the rocket exhaust. (BUNDESARCHIV BILD 101I-279-0940-19)

Panzerschreck

The German's improved bazooka

While the Panzerfaust is the most famous German anti-tank weapon of the war, the Panzerschreck comes in a close second. The name translates as 'tank terror,' and where the Panzerfaust was a single shot disposable weapon, the Panzerschreck could be reloaded and used repeatedly. Officially the weapon bore the designation RPzB54, or Raketenpanzerbüchse 54, which translates to 'Rocket Anti-Tank Rifle 54'.

The Panzerschreck bears a strong resemblance to the American bazooka because it is an enlarged copy of it. Many sources report examples of the bazooka captured in North Africa were sent to Germany for testing and inspired the Panzerschreck. However, the first bazookas captured by the Germans came from the Eastern Front, from a shipment of bazookas sent to the Soviet Union as military aid. Weapons taken in both locations were no doubt sent back to Germany, so the point is academic.

A primary reason for the Panzerschreck's larger 88mm calibre (the bazooka is a 60mm weapon) was due to an existing 88mm rocket round in use with a small wheeled anti-tank weapon called the Raketenwerfer 43 Puppchen. The rocket projectile from that weapon was modified to work in a bazooka-like launcher. This gave the Panzerfaust significantly better armour penetration than the bazooka, but it also created more smoke when fired, revealing the firer's location. In action Panzerschreck teams usually moved immediately after firing, just as bazooka teams did.

Unlike the bazooka, where the rocket was designed to use all its propellant before leaving the tube,

RIGHT: A group of German paratroopers equipped for tank-hunting, with a Panzerschreck and Panzerfaust 60. They are moving past a destroyed M4A3 Sherman in Normandy, 1944. (POLISH NATIONAL ARCHIVES)

RPzB54 Panzerschreck	
Calibre	88mm
Length	65in (1.64m)
Weight	24lb (11kg)
Effective Range	490ft (150m)
Penetration	Up to 230mm

the Panzerschreck rocket continued burning for a few yards out of the tube. To protect firers from the heat and blast, they were trained to wear protective clothing, including a gas mask, heavy gloves, and a heavy cover over their uniform. However, given the chaotic nature of combat, not all users always had these items as they could be lost or discarded. Many Panzerschrecks had a small shield to help protect the firer.

As temperature affects the volatility of propellants, the Germans developed different rockets for high and low temperatures. The high-temperature rocket was meant to operate in 40-50°C in the summer months. The low temperature version

ABOVE: A Panzerschreck crew loads their weapon in Italy, April 1944. They have a grenade and submachine gun close at hand. The firer will have to rise to fire to prevent the backblast from hitting the rear wall of the trench. (BUNDESARCHIV BILD 101I-313-1003-16A)

LEFT: A loader holds the Panzerschreck's 88mm rocket at the ready for a quick reload in Ukraine, March 1944. (BUNDESARCHIV BILD 101I-710-0371-25)

could remain operational in -25°C. However, users likely used whatever was at hand in combat. The designers estimated the Panzerschreck had a life of about a thousand rounds.

A simple sighting system on the weapon's left side could be adjusted for 100, 150 or 200 metres. A handle with a trigger, safety and shoulder brace were spaced along the bottom of the tube. Each Panzerschreck crew consisted of a gunner and loader who also carried spare rockets. Users were taught to limit their targets to tanks as the round had little fragmentation effect.

In action the weapon was effective and widely issued to infantry regiments. Allied tank crews certainly feared and respected them just as they did the Panzerfaust, although a report by German General Guderian

on the Eastern Front from January to April 1944, found the Panzerfaust responsible for three times the tank kills of the Panzerschreck. This was possibly due to the wider distribution and ease of use of the Panzerfaust, however.

Like the Panzerfaust, the Panzerschreck proved most effective at close range where a nervous gunner had a better chance of a hit. One American armoured unit found Panzerschreck attacks most effective at 50 metres or less during action in France. They also noted most Panzerfaust attacks missed at ranges above 20 metres. German doctrine placed Panzerschreck teams about 150 metres apart so they had overlapping coverage and could shoot at the side or rear armour of enemy tanks as they passed.

LEFT: An American soldier holds up a Panzerschreck and an M1 bazooka in comparison. The size difference is evident. (NARA)

Panzerfaust

Panzerfaust	
Calibre	100-106mm
Length	3.43ft (104.5cm)
Weight	6-15lbs (2.7-7kg)
Effective Range	30-150m based on type
Penetration	5.5-13in (140-320mm)

out the rear of the tube. This created a significant backblast behind the firer which would kick up dirt, dust and debris. This cloud would reveal the position of the firer, just as with other AT weapons like the Panzerschreck and bazooka. According to the weapon's instructions, this backblast was deadly to anyone standing within three metres of the firer and dangerous to anyone within ten metres. The tube had the warning 'Beware fire jet' in German at its rear to remind troops of the danger.

ABOVE: A member of the Berlin Volkssturm practices with a Panzerfaust. Late in the war, Volkssturm troops sometimes had no weapons except the Panzerfaust. (BUNDESARCHIV_BILD_183-J31390)

The Panzerfaust ('armour fist') is one of the most recognisable anti-tank (AT) weapons of World War Two. Almost 8.3 million of these one shot AT launchers were produced during the war and they were widely used by German troops on all fronts. In the last months of the war, Volkssturm militia sometimes received the Panzerfaust as their only weapon, lacking even rifles. Allied troops encountered them frequently and tank crews considered them a deadly threat at close range.

The weapon combined several relatively new design concepts, including a shaped charge warhead, and a recoilless launch tube. The Panzerfaust combined this simple launch tube with the warhead attached to the front of the tube and protruding from it. A rudimentary leaf site folded down against the tube until raised for firing. The user tucked the tube under their arm and held the Panzerfaust at an upward angle while aiming. Upon firing, the warhead flew from the tube towards the target, with four stabilising fins unfolding from the rear of the warhead. After firing, the tube was discarded and the user would have to retrieve a new weapon rather than reloading the tube.

As a recoilless weapon, much of the gas produced by firing was directed

RIGHT: Finnish infantry with Panzerfausts move past the wreckage of a Soviet T34 tank in June 1944. The tank either suffered an ammunition explosion or was demolished to prevent recovery. (SA-KUVA)

While the weapon is generally known as the Panzerfaust, it was produced in several versions. The first model entered service in 1943 and was initially called the Faustpatrone, or 'fist cartridge.' This smaller model used a 100mm warhead with armour penetration of up to 140mm. The Panzerfaust 30 soon replaced it and further developments results in the Panzerfaust 60, 100 and 150. These numbers designated the range of each model, i.e., the Panzerfaust 60 had an effective range of 60 metres. The 30, 60 and 100 could penetrate up to 200mm of armour and used a 149mm warhead. The Panzerfaust 60 was the most common type, while the Panzerfaust 150 was only made in small numbers for troop trials in 1945 just before Germany surrendered.

In combat use, the Panzerfaust required the firer to get close to their target; even 100 metres is easy range for enemy troops with rifles and machine guns. After firing they had to move quickly as the backblast likely revealed their location. A well-concealed soldier with a Panzerfaust posed a grave threat to an Allied tank, particularly in forested or urban terrain where cover and concealment were plentiful, and the distances close.

In 1943 and early 1944, the Panzerfaust was simply one AT weapon among many in the German arsenal. Accordingly, it accounted for a relatively small percentage of Allied tank losses.

However, as German fortunes waned in late 1944 and 1945, Panzerfausts began to account for a higher percentage of tank losses, as Germany ran out of other weapons such as anti-tank guns and their own armour. However, Panzerfausts accounted for only 11.7% of American tank losses in 1944 and 11.4% in 1945. By comparison, mines were responsible for 16.4 and 18.2% of tank losses respectively. This indicates the Panzerfaust had a distinct psychological effect which exceeded its actual performance.

A report by the American 736th Tank Battalion noted how the Panzerfaust could be used effectively in concert with other weapons. The report stated: "Resistance encountered was mainly at defended roadblocks and towns. Bazookas and Panzerfausts caused most of the trouble... the Germans would disable the tank by Panzerfaust... forcing the crew to abandon the tank. When the crews attempt to abandon the tanks, they would be shot at with machine pistols or machine guns."

In the hands of a competent and aggressive soldier, the Panzerfaust could be deadly. Heinrich Zubrod rose through the ranks of the German army to become an officer. In December 1944 -January 1945, as a lieutenant, Zubrod knocked out 13 tanks with Panzerfausts. Four of these tanks were knocked out on the same day and most of the tanks he engaged were from the French 5th Armoured Division. Zubrod received a Knight's Cross for his aggressive soldiering but died in action less than a month later.

Halftracks

Early in the war the major armies realised tanks needed the close support of infantry to be most effective and for protection from the enemy's anti-tank guns and infantry anti-tank teams. In 1939-41, there were a few half-track designs in existence, though only a tiny number saw service as infantry transports; most were used as towing vehicles for artillery and anti-aircraft guns. The majority of infantry in armoured units used lorries, though these had trouble keeping up with the tanks when moving cross country and had no armour protection.

Halftracks provided limited protection and better cross-country performance. They remained in wide use as tractors for guns and equipment but quickly became a preferred means of transport for mechanised infantry. Only Germany and the United States produced them in large numbers and the American models proliferated through Lend-Lease to the UK and Commonwealth forces, the Soviet Union, Free French Forces and others.

The lack of armour proved the halftrack's major disadvantage. Open-topped, they lacked overhead protection from artillery and mortar bursts. Their side armour would only stop medium machine gun fire at 200-300 metres.

The German halftracks were a little better in this regard as they had slightly thicker armour, some of which was sloped. US infantry often referred to their halftracks as 'Purple Heart Boxes', a reference to the American award for wounds received in combat.

SdKfz 251. This German halftrack design served as their primary infantry carrier, although few German units ever had enough to fully equip their mechanised infantry, known as Panzergrenadiers. The rest made do with lorries, rode on the tanks, or walked. This vehicle is often referred to as the Hanomag, after the name of the primary manufacturer. Each carried a squad of troops and had one or two MG34 or MG42 machine guns mounted for supporting fires and air defence. Many variants existed, including mortar carriers, command vehicles, and carriers for light cannon, anti-aircraft guns, and artillery rockets.

US Halftracks. The United States developed numerous models of Halftrack, with the base models designated the M2, M3, M5 and M9. As with the German models, many

variants existed, with the mortar and anti-aircraft versions being the ones most used to support infantry. The variants usually got their own model numbers; for example, the M16 halftrack carried a quad .50-calibre machine gun mounting frequently used with deadly effect against ground troops.

American armoured infantry used the M3, which usually had .50 and .30-calibre machine guns mounted to support its infantry squad. British

infantry in armoured divisions used halftracks less than their American counterparts, partly because they were already equipped with Universal Carriers. British units frequently used halftracks for supporting roles, such as towing anti-tank guns.

As the M3 and SdKfz 251 were the most widely used, they are often compared. The German model did have an advantage in armour protection, only slight, but important to anybody riding in one. However, the US M3 proved superior in most other respects. The M3's boxy body had 20% more internal volume. The M3 also had a powered front axle and 25% more horsepower; the SdKfz 251's front wheels were only for steering. The German halftrack's suspension was more complex and maintenance intensive, and the overlapping road wheels were more easily clogged with mud or debris. One US study found the M3 had better cross-country performance and a quieter suspension.

Late in the war the US and UK experimented with fully tracked personnel carriers, often converted from light and medium tanks.

ABOVE: Both sides used captured halftracks. This US M3, now in German hands, is following a Panzer VI Tiger in Tunisia, January 1943. (BUNDESARCHIV BILD 101I-557-1018-28A)

LEFT: A German SdKfz 251 on the Eastern Front, 1942. An SdKfz 250 reconnaissance halftrack is in the background and the machine gun team in the foreground seems ready for action, as the assistant has his pistol drawn. (BUNDESARCHIV BILD 101I-792-0138-21A)

LEFT: Two British Army halftracks on the road to Montchamp, France, August 1944. British forces were one of the major users of US halftracks. (IWM B8608)

US Marine War Dogs

While dogs saw service around the world, some of the most famous were the war dogs employed by the United States Marine Corps in the Pacific Theatre. Marines used these dogs as sentries against enemy infiltrators on the front lines.

They also served well as scouts, able to smell nearby Japanese troops. One officer called them 'living radar,' able to detect enemy soldiers a quarter-mile (400m) away.

Aside from serving as scouts and guards, war dogs carried messages between units and searched for

isolated or wounded Marines. Sometimes they carried medical supplies such as blood plasma and bandages. Marines with a dog nearby could sleep better, knowing the dog would warn them of an approaching threat. No Marine unit was ambushed when a dog was present. One dog, a German Shepherd named Caesar, pointed out so many enemy positions the Japanese made a concerted effort to kill him. Wounded, Caesar went back to the United States to recuperate and then helped sell war bonds. Many other dogs died.

The dogs performed such effective service other Marines gladly dug foxholes for them. On Okinawa, a dog named Prince smelled Japanese hiding under cut sugar cane, allowing his patrol to wipe them out with automatic weapons. Another

dog named Sampson attacked the Japanese himself, facing a Banzai charge, and on one occasion chasing down a Japanese soldier who hit him on the head and ran away.

After the war, the dog handlers and trainers could not bear the thought of the dogs being killed, so a retraining program was created at Camp Lejeune, a Marine Corps base in North Carolina. After a year-long stay, the dogs returned to life with civilian families, with no reports of them biting or injuring anyone.

ABOVE: Karl, a Doberman Pinscher of the 6th War Dog Platoon, checks a cave on Iwo Jima. If Japanese are present the dog would give an alert signal. Other Marines would then attack the cave with grenades, flamethrowers or explosives. (USMC)

ABOVE LEFT: A Doberman Pinscher named Dutch stands guard while his handler sleeps on Iwo Jima, February 1945. (US NAVY)

LEFT: Not all dogs in the war zone were war dogs. Most young men love dogs, and Marines are no exception. This Marine tank crewman adopted a litter of puppies on Okinawa and gave them 'Japanese' names, including Nancy, Shoto, Sake, Zero, Banzai and Okinawa. (USMC)

Glossary

The language of weaponry

Armoured Infantry	US term for mechanised infantry. These troops travelled in halftracks and were nicknamed 'armoured doughs', derived from the World War One nickname 'doughboys'.
AT	Anti-Tank.
BAR	Browning Automatic Rifle, standard US light machine gun.
Bipod	a two-legged stand usually used on a light machine gun or mortar to provide firing stability.
Bomb	correct term for a round of mortar ammunition.
Buckshot	pellets fired from a shotgun cartridge, often called a shell. The most common type, 00 Buck ('double-aught'), contained nine to 11 pellets of about .30-calibre.
Carbine	A compact rifle, usually a smaller version of a standard rifle. By World War Two, many infantry rifles were carbine versions of older weapons.
En-bloc clip	A small metal clip that was inserted into the rifle along with the cartridges it held. It was usually ejected from the weapon after the last round was fired.
HMG	Heavy Machine Gun.
Lanyard	a short cord tied to a pistol, with the other end tied to the user's belt or placed around their neck. It prevented the pistol from being lost during movement in combat.
LMG	Light Machine Gun.
Long Range Desert Group	A British Special Operations unit that conducted unconventional missions in North Africa.
MMG	Medium Machine Gun.
Monopod	a single leg stand used on some mortars and anti-tank rifles to provide firing stability.
OSS	Office of Strategic Services, an Anglo-American covert warfare group.
Sear Pin	A small pin in a weapons mechanism that holds the hammer or bolt in place until the trigger is squeezed.
SMG	Submachine Gun, a compact shoulder weapon firing pistol calibre ammunition.
SMLE	Short Magazine Lee-Enfield, the British No 1 Mk III rifle. Often pronounced 'Smelly'.
SOE	Special Operations Executive, a British covert warfare group.
Sturmgewehr	German for Assault Rifle. Germany fielded the first practical assault rifle during World War Two, giving its name to the type.
Tankodesantniki	Soviet infantry who rode tanks into battle, dismounting once engaged to protect the tanks.
Tripod	a three-legged stand used on machine guns to provide firing stability and allow the weapon to traverse across its assigned field of fire.

PHOTO CREDITS:

Asahigraph Pubic Domain, Australian War Memorial, Brasilian Archives, British Army, Bundesarchiv (German Federal Archive), Chinese Archives, Dutch National Archives, Finnish Heritage Society, IJA (Japan Public Domain), Imperial War Museum (IWM), Jewish National Fund, Library and Archives Canada, Library of Congress, Moscow Archives, Patton Museum, Polish National Archives, RIAN, Russian Archives, Russian MoD, SA-Kuva (Finnish Archives), NARA (US National Archives and Records Administration), US Marine Corps, US Navy, Zelenograd Museum.

BELOW: A BAR gunner fires his weapon, nicknamed 'Bertha'. (NARA)